Crosscurrents

Modern Critiques

New Series

Edited by
HARRY T. MOORE
and
MATTHEW J. BRUCCOLI

James Gould
Cozzens

New Acquist of True Experience

Edited by

Matthew J. Bruccoli

Southern Illinois University Press
Carbondale and Edwardsville

Feffer & Simons, Inc.
London and Amsterdam

Library of Congress Cataloging in Publication Data
Main entry under title:

James Gould Cozzens.

(Crosscurrents/modern critiques/new series)
Bibliography: p.
1.   Cozzens, James Gould, 1903-1978—Criticism
and interpretation—Addresses, essays, lectures.
I.   Bruccoli, Matthew Joseph, 1931-
PS3505.099Z69   813'.5'2   79-14581
ISBN 0-8093-0930-0

. . . that little miracle of making data on one particular human life relate constantly to what the reader's own life will have taught him, so that in following hers he is again and again receiving for himself nothing less than Milton's new acquist of true experience.

James Gould Cozzens to Gordon S. Haight,
15 September 1968

Contents

Notes on Contributors   ix

Introduction   xi
Matthew J. Bruccoli

1 The Complex World of James Gould Cozzens   1
   Louis Coxe

2 James Gould Cozzens: The Condition of Modern Man   15
   John William Ward

3 Cozzens and the Conservative Spirit   29
   Pierre Michel

4 Moral Realism: The Development of an Attitude   44
   Robert Scholes

5 The Title of *The Last Adam*   63
   Colin S. Cass

6 *Guard of Honor:* Providential Luck in a Hard-Luck   81
   World
   R. H. W. Dillard

7 The Particularity of *Guard of Honor*   92
   R. V. Cassill

8 The Novelist as Professional   99
   Bernard De Voto

9 Nomination for a Nobel Prize   102
   John Fischer

10 Henry Dodd Worthington: The "I" in *Morning Noon and*   111
   Night
   Leland H. Cox, Jr.

11 Statements on James Gould Cozzens   127
   Malcolm Cowley, James Dickey, Orville Prescott,
   Joseph Slatter, C. P. Snow, Edward Weeks, Jerome
   Weidman

   Notes   137

   The Publications of James Gould Cozzens   142

Notes on Contributors

MATTHEW J. BRUCCOLI, Jefferies Professor of English at the University of South Carolina, is editor of the Lost American Fiction series. His latest book is *Just Representations: A James Gould Cozzens Reader.*

COLIN S. CASS teaches American literature at Wayne State University. He wrote his doctoral dissertation on Cozzens's early fiction.

R. V. CASSILL is a novelist, short story writer, and critic. He has taught at Columbia, University of Iowa, Purdue, and Harvard and is now Professor of English at Brown. His most recent novel is *Hoyt's Child.*

LELAND H. COX, JR., is the Executive Director of the South Carolina Committee for the Humanities.

LOUIS COXE, Pierce Professor of English at Bowdoin College, is a critic, playwright, and poet. His latest books are *Enabling Acts* and *Passage-Selected Poems.*

BERNARD DE VOTO, author of nearly a score of books dealing with history and literature, won the Pulitzer Prize for history and the National Book Award for nonfiction. He served as editor of major magazines and conducted the "Easy Chair" for *Harper's Magazine.* He died in 1955.

R. H. W. DILLARD, Professor of English and Chairman of the creative writing program at Hollins College in Virginia, is a poet, novelist, and critic. His most recent books are *After Borges, The Book of Changes,* and *Horror Films.*

JOHN FISCHER, editor and writer, contributed to many major American periodicals. He was Washington correspondent for A.P. and foreign correspondent for U.P.I., covering England and Germany. From 1953 to 1967 he was editor of *Harper's Magazine.* He died in 1978.

PIERRE MICHEL, Associate Professor of American literature and Director of Centre d'Enseignement et de Recherche en Etudes Américaines at Liège University, is the author of *James Gould Cozzens* and of *J. G. Cozzens: An Annotated Checklist.*

ROBERT SCHOLES, Professor of English at Brown University, has written a number of books on narrative literature and modern fiction, including *Elements of Fiction, Elements of Poetry,* and *Structural Fabulation: An Essay on Fiction of the Future.*

JOHN WILLIAM WARD, former President of Amherst College, is the author of *Andrew Jackson: Symbol for an Age* and of *Red, White, and Blue: Men, Books, and Ideas in American Culture.*

Introduction

MATTHEW J. BRUCCOLI

James Gould Cozzens dismissed most contemporary literary criticism as "attempts to find what isn't there," holding that writers who write accurately and truthfully require no exegetical help. Moreover, he insisted that he cared nothing about his posthumous reputation and very little about the contemporary reception of his books. He was content to be read by the people who understood his aims, and he resisted attempts to make him a literary figure. Fame was not the spur, and he found the enormous success of *By Love Possessed* embarrassing—suspecting that he was in danger of being taken up by the weak-minded. Cozzens wrote books because he was a born writer, although appalled by the literary life. Henry Dodd Worthington's remarks on the profession of authorship in *Morning Noon and Night* are instructive:

> I am prepared to believe that the life term at hard labor of serious writing, the disappointments of normal early failure, the discouragements of likewise normal continued unsuccess over months and years, the active large and small nastinesses of the undercover melee, the slings and arrows of enemy criticism's addictive lying, and the poor financial pickings that are the average professional's ordinary lot can none of them, or all of them together, nonplus in the least a person with the true urge to write, the writer born. If you shy away, you aren't that person, you weren't meant to be a writer.

In terms of Cozzens's protocols, then, this volume seems uncalled for. It is justified by the circumstance that he wrote for publication and therefore for readers. Although Cozzens rejected as unfit readers "everyone who could not or would not meet heavy demands on his attention and intelligence, or lacked the imagination to grasp a large pattern and the wit to see the relation which I could not stop to spell out between this & that," it is the function of literary criticism to preserve the best literature by assisting the intelligent, attentive, and perceptive reader to find out what is there. And James Gould Cozzens was one of the best American novelists.

Cozzens knew about this project—which began in 1977, while he was still alive—and gave it his restrained approval. His position was that he didn't want it, but felt that it would be uncivil and ungrateful for him to oppose the efforts of people who respected his work. A personal note may be proper here in view of the fact that Cozzens's public image was that of an extremely difficult man—"the hermit of Lambertville" as *Time* put it. I worked with Jim Cozzens for six years on various publishing projects. He was always generously helpful and, after a while, a warm friend. Of course he protected his privacy: there is no requirement that a writer be a celebrity or behave like one. It took all of Cozzens's time to write according to his own standards.

As these essays demonstrate, Cozzens's work can be legitimately enlarged or made more accessible to fit readers by sensible criticism. Cozzens wrote and rewrote for clarity and precision, but his novels are complexly designed works by a writer of high intelligence and wide learning. The equipped reader will get most of it for himself, but professional help may well enable him to comprehend more.

An approach to Cozzen's fiction is provided by a phrase from *Samson Agonistes* that he savored in his later years: "new acquist of true experience." Cozzens regarded himself as a realist and only that, holding that his task was to record conduct with minute fidelity, eschewing all attempts to impose messages beyond the insistence that life is what life is: "I don't defend anything; I don't eagerly assert anything." What his novels reveal about the limitations of reason develops from his accurate observation of life. As he noted in his journal in 1960, "My writing aim would be not so much to tell the reader new things as to remind him what he knows." But at the same time that he was committed to rendering life truthfully, he was concerned about the limits of realism—that is, the problem of writing fiction from true experience that provides the reader with new acquist of true experience through the structuring and ordering of material. In 1944, while he was considering ways to use his Air Force experience in the fiction, he commented in his journal: "The difficulty a writer has in doing things all of a piece is one of our great literary problems—at what point in realism do you add imagination to fact, and why?" He wrote truthfully by avoiding the varieties of imagination that he saw mistaken for profundity or deep feeling or transcending insight in the work of others. When in 1960 Cozzens came across an article that praised Popeye of Faulkner's *Sanctuary* as an "original" character in contrast with Arthur Winner of *By Love Possessed* as a "copy," Cozzens's response in his journal was:

> Look, Stupid. It's a copy, all right. That's the whole point of writing fiction for grown-up readers. The copy is from life. Anyone who knows, or moves in, the described circles recognizes him. The whole point about created "original" characters is that no one ever saw them. They're by definition strictly on paper, and an intelligent reader (as opposed to literary intellectuals making a cult of the abstract and impressionistic) soon sees there's no reason to waste his reading time that way.

The essays assembled here do not cover the entire Cozzens canon. They offer worthwhile critical approaches and indicate useful areas for further examination. During his life the reputation-makers never knew what to do about Cozzens. Mostly they ignored him—which did not bother him because he wanted nothing that was in their power to grant. But the quarantining of Cozzens deprived many readers of the rich experience of reading him. The long process of reappraisal has commenced. When it is accomplished the novels of James Gould Cozzens will be secure among the enduring achievements of American literature.

1

LOUIS COXE

The Complex World of
James Gould Cozzens[1]

"IT'S HARD to explain what I mean," says Francis Ellery, the young writer who is the chief character of *Ask Me Tomorrow.* "The situation is ironic, but also heroic. I don't think I can explain." What Francis doesn't think he can do, Cozzens undertakes to do for him and for the readers of most of Cozzens's novels. For if one can say with any certainty that there is *a* theme for the best of the books, it would seem to be this: the double vision of modern man, the central paradox of action and contemplation, of understanding and conduct, of the ironic view and the heroic efficacy.

That such a theme has concerned many writers of our age a short view of the literature evidences. With most novelists, however, we become aware that the attempt is to describe the split between the worlds of action and thought, or to celebrate the one as opposed to the other. *The Magic Mountain* redresses the balance overset by *The Sun Also Rises; The Sound and the Fury* supplies the lack we feel after *A Passage to India;* suffering from *The Portrait of the Artist as a Young Man,* we later find a cure, perhaps, in Graham Greene's *The End of the Affair.* In each reaction from the previous action, we are as readers victims of polarities, willing ones to be sure, but nonetheless victims. It has been, I think, the peculiar contribution of Cozzens to the twentieth-century novel that what goes on in his books is a dramatization of experience within that whole gamut stretching between the poles, the region of our experience, the places in which we live and die and work. And of course there is nothing new in this, though much of it has been forgotten. Cozzens is the legitimate heir of George Eliot and, nearer to our own day, of Conrad. However pedestrian or exotic the worlds of the novels of these two writers, the question usually resolves itself thus: What do these people *do* and what strange concatenation of luck, logic, and living has brought them to this pass? Within the huge area thus described lies the central question of will and the drama of the will's formation, exercise, and ultimate dependence. With few expressed assumptions as to the proper conduct of life in general, Cozzens creates a world of particulars, a world of men and women at their tasks and duties, and then tries to show the intricacy of the web of will and desire, and stuff of action, as these work out in men's involvement with one another, with themselves, with their tasks—all of these relationships described with irony, shown in action, brought to a climax best characterized as heroic.

General statements of this sort are of little use without a full knowledge of the novels themselves, and I fear that Cozzens has fewer readers than he deserves, largely because there are difficulties in the way of an estimate of worth, difficulties of fashion and technique, and even more than these, difficulties of basic assumption about the nature of the world and the point of vantage from which one observes the world. Cozzens has few companions in our time, among novelists at least; among poets E. A. Robinson shares certain attributes with him. All this seems to indicate something that should be stressed by any critic of Cozzens: his entire method and technique have an appearance of old-fashioned discursiveness, of a certain formidable denseness of surface best described, again, as old-fashioned.

Not that Cozzens's novels, with the exception of *Guard of Honor,* are very long; most say what they need to say in the (formerly) canonical 300 pages or thereabouts. Nor does Cozzens overwhelm us with realistic detail or delicately conceived and highly wrought personal insights. On the whole, the form and texture of these novels are traditional, conservative, and uncomplicated. The trouble lies just there: expecting certain kinds of formal qualities which in turn create the further expectancy of finding certain sorts of meaning, we are deterred at the very start by a sensibility which, being tough, demands toughness. We can fit Cozzens nowhere into the survey course. He sees through our feelings, and we do not like it. For like most of the characters in most of the novels, we cling to what we know, fearing the loss of identity that comes with the double vision. Like Francis Ellery, cursed with a sense of complexity, we would go just so far and then turn back when the going gets tough; perhaps unlike Francis, most of us make the turn with—well, if not success, at least ease.

Initiation into the world of complexity, not mere complication, is then one aspect of Cozzens's scheme, and for most of his heroes there is the constant struggle with fact and with self. Many of the protagonists are men of mature age—Ross in *Guard of Honor,* Dr. Bull in *The Last Adam,* Ernest Cudlipp in *Men and Brethren*—and these characters in their various ways have worked out for themselves a mode of action and a standard of conduct by which they judge others and by which we as readers may judge them. They have passed the age when character may be said to be forming still; it is now a question of what is to be done with the life thus set, and of course Cozzens sees that life as one of profession, work, and of the vision a man has of himself and the work he does. Colonel Ross, with his trained legal mind and his trained use of the double vision, can play his Chiron to General Beal's Achilles—the ironist to the hero—and in the course of three days can make a mature man out of a hot pilot. He can work this miracle because all things work together for complexity for those able to see it and—do something with it. If in the gathering excitement of *Guard of Honor* the more critical of us think we must be on guard against the meretricious, against a *Caine Mutiny,* we would do well to think here of Conrad in *Nostromo.* If on the other hand we look in Cozzens's novels for kinds of techniques and styles we tend to associate with significant writing, we should remember, for example, Milton: the fact that a writer does not write a certain way does not mean he cannot. The Faulknerian purple patch or the rhapsodies of *nada* and sleeping bag may not be beyond a writer's powers; they may be simply outside his purposes. The gross stimulant of the idiosyncratic has a proper function in art, but that function is ephemeral; George Borrow and Ronald Firbank do not necessarily cure what ails us any better than Henry James and G. B. Shaw. Often what captures us in a writer is the sense of power in reserve, of potency. We know that Milton could and did write a "Comus" and do not therefore say that a further exploration of the vein was beyond his powers. We can read *Paradise Lost* or *Samson Agonistes* and consider a few masques well forgone for this gift.

Power in potency as well as in efficacy—this Cozzens preeminently has. Here is God's plenty—in range of action and feeling, in virile prose style, in setting, in character, in humor. Do you like novels of great scope and variety? Try *Guard of Honor.* Do you like the packed, delicate analytic work of insight into character and moral decision? *Ask Me Tomorrow* should satisfy. Do you prefer a realistic treatment of ordinary folk going about their lives and ways, yet with a heightened awareness? *The Just and the Unjust* should answer. In all these books Cozzens dramatizes significant action while he gives a sense of power in reserve and varies pace and tone so adeptly as to convey a sense of mastery, of mature, unself-conscious command of the medium almost unique in American fiction. The irony does not destroy the heroism, nor does the heroic purpose annihilate the complexity.

Such achievement is, as Cozzens observes through the sensibility of Miro in *S.S. San Pedro*, "a matter of *tela*, of form." That fatal word, *form*. I believe that preeminently among contemporary writers Cozzens has rediscovered aspects of form, of the formal observances that constitute the good manners of fiction, which most of us have not found lately and have therefore stopped looking for in a way; the sense has begun to atrophy. And since the appetite for art is artificial, cultivated, art itself can lose attributes that make it the more artful while we search for glossier trim; the gross stimulant of rhetoric, in lieu of style, makes us perhaps insensitive to real prose, the kind of prose that avoids excesses and ranges back and forth between the poles of bare simplicity and a highly wrought complexity—never, though, resting at the poles themselves. Such a style Cozzens commands: avoidance of extremes without either insipidity or dullness; it is only thus that a novelist can keep his style supple, useful for many purposes. It is, I believe, the triumph of the fine novelist that he be able to suggest boredom without boring, dullness without dulling, tumidity without flatulence. It is "a matter of *tela*, of form." Things are "going as they should go—tight, smart." And above all, someone is doing a job of work, for a purpose, for delight, for wisdom, in many tones of voice and between the hysterical poles where lies the country of universal human experience. It is a multivocal tone. If one wants strict point of view, *Ask Me Tomorrow* will provide that, but in a sense the problem of form in these novels is denser than a consideration of what tricks can be played. We can look at it this way: among contemporary novelists Cozzens is unique in the use of a ratiocinative technique superimposed on a dramatic, almost melodramatic, subject matter, and one of the excitements of the best work derives from the tension vibrating between these seeming irreconcilabilities. For example, in *Guard of Honor* the first section of the novel moves back and forth in time while the actual chronological duration of the focal situation consumes some four hours; we meet many of the important characters; the heroic exploits of Bus Beal are thrillingly recounted, spiced with the appropriate ironic comment in the mind of Ross, the ratiocinative observer whose sensibility and speculative intelligence control the tone and meaning; and the section ends with the near-catastrophe at the landing field, the slugging of the Negro pilot, and the breaking of a violent thunderstorm. Throughout we are aware of where we are—in an airplane over inland Florida. Cozzens creates with care and economy the spare, functional setting and the general ambience compounded of technical detail, rumor of war, and the relativity of time.

The atmosphere thus set persists throughout the book. One of the ironies in this heroic narrative derives from the juxtaposition of the petty and the vast—a motif that expresses itself in opposition of character, of incident, and of mood. All the people in this book do things—there is a war on, and they have duties to perform, often in conflict with their desires and best gifts, but war and life exact their services. The better adjusted folk, the men of single vision, act their parts ritualistically, formally, like the master and technical sergeants of the Knock and Wait Club, whereas the complex, or potentially complex, characters must do and act in a welter of indecision, mixed motives, and self-scrutiny, like Ross and Hicks. It is one of the great affirmations of Cozzens's work that he knows his men of double vision for doers as well as seers—doers of evil at times, perhaps, but never mere self-pitying impotents letting I-dare-not wait upon I-would. They are men, living and trying to clean up the messes left by the grown-up adolescents with whom their lot is of necessity cast. As Ross observes, the guard of honor should be for the living, not for the dead. The empty ceremonies in which we engage in order to make palatable or attractive those tasks that would otherwise appall cannot satisfy men cursed with the double vision, those who, tragically perhaps and certainly ironically, must be the doers the very while that they see most clearly the magnitude of the work and the inadequacy of the tools, their own and everyone else's. Hence much of the overt irony revolves about the eternal point of the discrepancy between the way things look and the way they are, between reality as it must be taken if we are to live fully in it and reality as men so often corrupt it to make their delusions viable. And that Cozzens may the more dramatically vivify his multifarious theme, he peoples his story with characters whose relation to the theme is expressed by each one's degree of maturity, his awareness of things as they really are. Captain Andrews is a mathematical genius and a person of sweetness and simplicity, and his view of the world and of the nature of life is preposterous. General Nichols, that "stripped-down, comfortless, plain and simple mind," may from the rarefied height of his aloofness see the others as "superannuated children," may see that "Each childish adult determinedly bet his life and staked his sacred pride on, say, the Marxist's ludicrous substance of things only hoped for, or the Christian casuist's wishful evidence of things not so much as seen." Yet his is the simpler nature. In the end, the hot flyboy Bus Beal, who has come to the realization of complexity, has the last word, over Nichols and all the rest:

> "Jo-Jo [Nichols] thinks I need a nurse. That's you. I guess I do act that way." He laughed. "Don't worry, Judge," he said. He put his hand suddenly on Colonel Ross's shoulder. "Even Jo-Jo knows they could do without him before they could do without me. That's not boasting, Judge. There's a war on. Jo-Jo can talk to Mr. Churchill; but the war, that's for us. Without me—without us, he wouldn't have a whole hell of a lot to talk about, would he?"

He includes Ross with himself and himself with Ross. Attaining to the double vision without consequent loss of power means maturity for Beal—and responsibility. From now on, when he will act as he must, he must also say, with Ross, "I really saw nobody all day who was not in one way or another odious. . . . And, of course, in every situation, I was odious, too." Whether or not Mrs. Beal can emulate Mrs. Ross and say, " 'I know.' . . . She moved until her head rested against his shoulder. 'Let's not go on about it' "—that is perhaps uncertain. What the reader knows is that the guard of honor should indeed be for the living.

This novel is certainly Cozzens's most detailed, most complex dramatization of the complex theme; yet most of the others, each in its particular way, show the unending struggle of the main characters for unity within diversity, for a tough sense of the actual coupled with a love for life and people. One of the basic lessons Francis Ellery, in *Ask Me Tomorrow* must learn, in suffering and near-despair, is the lesson of human limitation, that you cannot eat your cake and have it too. Abner Coates, in *The Just and the Unjust,* goes to the same hard school. Cozzens does not pretend that school is fun and "learning-experiences"; it is, plainly, life, and though he does not minimize the pain and the humiliation, neither does he romanticize suffering nor celebrate solemnity. Cozzens's heroes are serious, not solemn, and they have humor or at least find humor and pleasure in their routines, their loves, their daily work. Living can be, for them, all of a piece because while their vision of the world is multiform, the incapacitating effect of such vision is forestalled by their delight in living and working—in their curiosity about people, their delight in the exercise of their own powers, in their fine sense of the rich surprise and humor of life. It amounts to love, love with a sense "of *tela,* of form."

Nowhere does this dense feeling for life emerge more clearly than in the style. I know of no modern novelist who commands such a range of idiom, allusion, cadence, rhetorical radiation and vocabulary. It is a muscular, virile style with certain strong affinities to seventeenth-century prose—Cozzens is fond of Bunyan, Milton, Defoe, among others. Yet one does not get the feeling of reading a "literary" novel. The ironic view alone prevents this. For the ordinary reader the allusiveness and learning serve two purposes: they give a sense of mind in operation and they remind him that the intellectual faculties are here taken seriously, as a vital part of living. Moreover, the method of Cozzens in this regard is to make both the learned allusion and its application appropriate to his character: Abner Coates does not show a great range of knowledge and erudition, though his father does, and properly so. Ernest Cudlipp, an Anglican priest, should and does have views on and, ideally at least, considerable scholarly knowledge of, Barthian theology, the Thirty-nine Articles, and the music of Bach. And it is not at all surprising that Colonel Ross, trained in the old school, should have by heart lines from *Samson Agonistes.* Cozzens does not, then, wish to impress us with his learning. What does impress us, however, is the flexibility of the style and mastery of tone that allow a writer to shift from the highly idiomatic speech of contemporary characters to allusive play while at the same time no violent wrenching, no destruction of tone, spoils matters for mind and ear alike. One could quote many characteristic passages, or present the magnificently comic yet pathetic scene of Francis Ellery's entrapment by Mr. McKellar, the learned amateur of all the arts, the incredible windbag. It is a devastating portrait and a scene dramatic with many shifts and shades, tonal and ironic. And throughout the style operates, not for and by itself, but accommodating itself to the situation and its tone, to the speaker, to the ones spoken to—and above all to the totality of the theme to be dramatized. I can do no better here than give three sentences describing, through Francis's sensibility, Mr. McKellar's discourse:

> With peans and apostrophes he contrasted the state of creatures living as nature meant them to, and of man, living as a foul and flagitious civilization dictated. Spoken by Mr. McKellar, the English language died in extremity, was solemnly buried, and rose again having put on incorruption. It became more English, not in the imitative sense of resembling an Englishman's speech—until Mr. McKellar took up his residence there such an accent could hardly ever have been heard in England—but absolutely, in the sense of resembling a Platonic ideal, with "a's" so nobly broad and feats of synaeresis so extraordinary that the most supercilious don would have to go down, and Mr. McKellar bore the palm alone.

It is high humor, and the diction (who since Pope has dared use that adjective "flagitious," even if he knew what it meant?) and the syntax take much of the credit for the effect. Cozzens's vocabulary is huge, its use precise, its tonal range satisfyingly various. He does not depend on the unusual word, the shock of lack of recognition. A passage of this sort, from *Guard of Honor,* shows what he can do with the simplest elements:

> Moderately warmed by whisky, Nathaniel Hicks took a look at the blonde girl on what might be called his own account; yet where Captain Wiley saw such a temptingly available delicacy, all Nathaniel Hicks saw was a lot of trouble. Reason, indeed, overcomes the passions! If, by lifting his finger now, he could enjoy her, would he lift it? He would not! He would go further than that. If—an improbable hypothesis, since he was not exactly Captain Wiley—the propositioning was hers; if she provided, with no work of finger-lifting, the necessary time and place to "organize" her; if she then and there offered herself to him, free of bother and uncertainty of going after her, would he accept? He felt safe in saying he would, instead, get the hell out the shortest way.

The possibilities for humor and contrast in such a stylistic tone are apparent; the general toughness of syntax, that masculine power which, though not drawing attention to itself is always there and shows itself on analysis, informs the best of all Cozzens's work. Whether one selects such a passage as that from *S.S. San Pedro* describing a vessel turning over her main engines at the pier, or something like the last paragraph of Section I of *Guard of Honor,* the enduring impression remains one of power, hard intellectuality, and humanity.

Style cannot divorce content satisfactorily; they stay married happily or unhappily. Cozzens has always chosen difficult subjects for his novels, and if it can be said that both vocabulary and syntax reflect and vivify the toughness of his thought, it can equally be declared that the increasing complexity of the worlds he chooses for the milieux of his novels augments the power of his theme. If one goes back to the quotation from *Ask Me Tomorrow,* one can see perhaps only a happy wit and a precise economy of style; in context, however, the passage has many overtones, for there we find another aspect of the theme of expatriate Americans, another ironic juxtaposition, another accentuation of the pathos of Francis's position, a further range of complexity in the allusion to a type. Mr. McKellar is—who? Ford Madox Ford? It scarcely matters, for we know *him,* whoever he may be.

What we continue increasingly to discover in these novels as they grow in maturity and depth is the constant theme of the heroic, and perhaps its converse, the craven. In *Castaway,* near-allegory; in *S.S. San Pedro,* a suggestion of symbolism, and a dramatization of the heroic, cheek by jowl with the ordinary, the craven, the simply dutiful. Yet after all, in the presentation of life as it strikes the sensibility and intellect of the novelist, what must occur if not the vision of reality and man's unceasing, seemingly unsuccessful attempt to cope with it? Reality viewed as the intractable given, about which nothing can be done and which we ignore at our peril—no high-flown peril to some impossibly delicate putative antennae, but to a man's livelihood, body, and immortal soul. And Cozzens's heroes fight for life, the life that old Judge Coates speaks for at the end of *The Just and the Unjust,* or which Ernest Cudlipp in *Men and Brethren* sees all about him, in a prurient elevator boy, an unfaithful wife, a shattered Alaskan missionary, a homosexual renegade monk. Life everywhere, and not good just because it is life, but always heroic when most it fulfills its true nature and makes for more and fuller life. And life has much meaning here: growth, maturity, wisdom, loving kindness, variousness, honor. Never abstract, these qualities come before us in the novels; we see the hero smug in his security gradually being stripped to—well, perhaps a General Nichols, but far better in the long run to a Francis Ellery or a Colonel Ross. Even as they go through their *peine forte et dure,* these latter come to accept and embrace the world. It is, finally, love; love with belief, and with belief both responsibility and the wisdom deriving therefrom.

Wisdom may be the answer for Cozzens and his heroes. Neither Achilles nor Hector, but Odysseus. In so far as a man lacks the capacity to enter into another's nature and understand it, at least partially, he lacks heroic stature; in so far as the man of vision is paralyzed by the baffling dimensions of that vision, he is the mere ironist: Dr. Bull in *The Last Adam,* is ultimately unsatisfying as a protagonist, as a hero, for his very lack of vision, as Mr. Banning in the same novel fails to satisfy as a foil to Bull because he lacks muscle to pursue his vision and make it workable in his life. He retreats into his money and his taste. Yet why not, really? That is the way things go in life. In the later novels, Cozzens does, I think, take a long stride ahead. Not content simply to show things as he sees them in their essence to be—in all their vital complexity of technique and demand for mastery or botch—he develops a suppler style and a more profound insight into the nature of vitality in its fullest sense. The worlds of the later novels—*Men and Brethren, The Just and the Unjust, Ask Me Tomorrow, Guard of Honor*—grow more complex, in step with the increasing richness of the minds of the characters, while the range of allusion and application broadens, and the technical detail becomes thicker, the life described denser. This capacity for growth has always been unusual in American writers; the fact that Cozzens has for one reason or another remained out of fashion and the public (or critical) eye may have contributed to this growth, and few will summon the dubious charity to wish him a sudden vogue.

Yet the question of a lack of serious attention to Cozzens's work cannot be set aside simply because one knows full well the damage done to American writers by an undeserved or disproportionate popularity; clearly the opposite danger has in our country done an equal amount of harm. If in this discussion of Cozzens's novels I have placed large emphasis on the intellectual elements in his work, I do not wish to imply that the novels are mere *contes philosophiques* or theses; I reiterate, if the method seems at times to be ratiocinative, speculative, analytic, the matter thus explored is nonetheless dramatic. From the beginning (ignoring those first ventures Cozzens himself would surely wish to expunge) the wedding of spiritual, physical, and moral crises has been his concern, and, of course, the desideratum of the more thoughtful critics of our time. What else have we asked for all these years in our art? Why do the book-reviewers continually call for some new Tolstoy who will bring together sweeping action and genuine theme? Why have we tired of those so terribly perceptive insight vendors, by James out of Ford? As Edmund Wilson pointed out not so very long ago, Kafka is not necessarily good for what ails us, nor should we complain when Mr. Wouk sweeps all before him; what else are we offered? In poetry we have fared better; the vitality we long to find has caught us up in the work of Yeats, Auden, the later Eliot. If we look to the novel for art as well as crudeness, sometimes confused with power, we are hard put to it to name anyone. We lament this state of affairs; the voices of J. Donald Adams and R. P. Blackmur are raised simultaneously if cacophonously, and everyone wants power, wisdom, moral vision. How else explain the Conrad revival? The rediscovery of Dickens and George Eliot? The awed admiration for *The Adventures of Augie March?* Casting about for some sign that the novel did not die while we dozed over *The Disguises of Love* and *The Groves of Academe,* we seize on any *big* (thick) book and after we have assured ourselves that it could not possibly suit Hollywood, we take comfort in the con-tinued existence of the old bourgeois epic. And all the time, quietly and with attention neither from Hollywood nor the literary quarter-lies, James Gould Cozzens has written at least three novels, perhaps four, to rank with the best of our time. Does this sound familiar? Did anything of this sort happen before? Hawthorne? Melville? Dickin-son? Robinson? It has happened before, and to the best of our artists. Why should it seem particular with them?

Fashion of course plays a major part, yet when one has said that, one needs to discover what elements in the prevailing or succeeding fashions have militated against the suitable reception of a fine novelist. Certainly Cozzens is far too complex and tough an author to appeal to a wide audience—in his own time, at any rate. As for the smaller audience—the one that reads Dylan Thomas, T. S. Eliot, and Robert Frost, the one that is eager to find out about good reading when it can be assured it is *good*—the smallest audience has not yet passed down the word on Cozzens. The smallest audience (critics, writers, even some professors) does not want to bother, having settled for Faulkner and Hemingway—and that should be enough for one generation. After all, Hemingway is set—the first and the last are the one book, and in his beginning is his end. We know all about it—or think we do. Myth. Ritual. Nada. Cojones. I have no intention of flinging mud at writers who cannot be smirched by such a foolish gesture; I would remark merely that we have overlooked a whole tradition, and the occasional attempts to recapture it have failed because we looked in the wrong places. The intense discipline of the craft of fiction that James and Conrad taught us to revere, and that we delight to throw over when we switch to Dreiser, has somehow led us to believe that high art cannot be dissociated from refinement, from sensibility perplexed in the extreme. Only lately have we come to the Conrad of *Nostromo;* it should not be much of a step to *Guard of Honor.* The chief difficulty lies in Cozzen's uncompromising refusal to mix genres and to simplify theme. He insists on writing prose and on pursuing the uneasy question of the lives *we live;* we can like it or lump it. This is not to say that no one has ever lived in the fashion of Studs Lonigan or of Milly Theale; it is simply that most of us rather take that on faith. In the case of Cozzen's novels we could use a little less faith and more simple understanding. His characters belong to trades and professions and towns and milieux the way Dickens's folk belong to some special way of living. If for the modern reader there is something of the exotic in a Chadband or a Wemmick, there need not necessarily have been such an appeal when *Bleak House* and *Great Expectations* first appeared. The exotic elements for the modern reader are nonetheless compelling; and in Cozzens's novels the world of types explored by Dickens and by Shaw and by Ben Jonson comes before us again in its unfamiliar shape—the shape of the local, urban, and workaday qualities too trivial to most novelists in recent years to seem worthy of their attention. Cozzens forces our attention, concentrates it, makes us inescapably aware of the density of the lives we lead.

The double vision, the awareness of complexity, affects not only style and character, but most important of all, action. I have mentioned the near-melodramatic tinge sometimes assumed by Cozzens's plots, but this tells us no more than that the books deal in incident piled on incident, in violence at times, and in large scenes of catastrophe: shipwreck and near-panic in *S.S. San Pedro,* a trial for murder in *The Just and the Unjust,* terror and the killing of a lunatic in *Castaway,* various episodes of death and near-death in *Guard of Honor.* In thus packing his novel with action, Cozzens again seems to be reverting to an old-fashioned conception of the milieu, to a conception with epic qualities. The purpose has more to do with the novelistic than the sociological; that is, I do not believe Cozzens is trying to tell us that modern life is violent and that modern novels should therefore show violence, though there may be much truth in such a contention. Nor is the purpose merely the exposition of the theme of good and evil. I think the answer lies, as I hope I have suggested, in a view at once simpler and more profound. He takes, a priori, the position that life is a tragic affair. The novel does not illustrate the view; rather, the action, in the Aristotelian sense, departs from this initial point, leaving it always there, as the given, the transparent window through which we view the unfolding action in its perspectives. Though this departure has elements of originality, Cozzens can nevertheless be reckoned the legitimate heir of Hawthorne and Melville, and perhaps of Poe. Unmistakably American in his peculiar moral vision, he refines on the rationale of many American writers by taking as the very base and fabric of that vision, and the cosmology it would observe, a sternly Calvinistic (with qualifications) measure of grace, salvation, and works. Whether his knowledge of seventeenth-century writers contributes to this attitude I cannot say; in any event, the Melville of *Billy Budd* and the Hawthorne of "Young Goodman Brown" would find no difficulty with these novels. And I am sure that Poe would envy Cozzens *Castaway* and much of *Guard of Honor*. Moral obliquity, the question of salvation by grace or by works, or by neither, the problem of power and its necessity—these are central issues in the work of our best writers and Cozzens takes them as given. Within the mode of the realistic novel he contrives a single action to which all characters and incidents relate; as we see the complexities arise we involve ourselves in the world of these characters, but we do not at any point empathize to a degree destructive of the basic assumption—to the point at which we are able to say comfortingly to ourselves: "Everything is relative." Cozzens forces us to look unflinchingly at the relativity of all things, at degrees of justice and injustice, for example, and Abner Coates, the young attorney, works out his destiny between the poles of total rejection of responsibility and assumption of a cynical relativism. He is neither Goodman Brown nor Captain Delano. It may be that his father is a sort of Captain Vere. For most of Cozzens's characters of heroic stature, the nature of the Shavian "Master of reality" becomes the object of their struggle. The novels move outward with the quest for reality, vision, and direction.

The descriptive term old-fashioned comes to a very great deal more, ultimately, than the matter of techniques. The traditional view of American writers, much discussed in our own time but rarely dramatized in literature, takes shape in Cozzens's novels. Of course it is idle to force the point and play games of reducing all American novels to two types, the Huck and the Ahab, pleasant occupation though it may be. For one thing, Cozzens is far more at home in his world of fact and technique than ever Melville and Hawthorne could be; the temptation towards allegory, which they could never resist, Cozzens transmutes in his best work into an urge for complex vision. He has found in a man's work and his means of objectifying his desires the mythos or world view comfortable and appropriate to his gift. That he has grown and matured in power and profundity seems proof of this: from May Tupping of *The Last Adam* to Ross of *Guard of Honor,* his masters of reality deepen in understanding and compassion while their view of the world multiplies its vistas to conform with the increased size of the stage they must occupy and try to dominate. None of these characters loses awareness of self for all the awareness of the dangers of self-pity. Humor remains at the worst of times; however catastrophic the event may prove, there is always the trying and the illimitable curiosity; understanding and belief will come from the trying, given luck and as much good management as a man is capable of. As Judge Coates says at the very end of *The Just and the Unjust,* "We just want you to do the impossible." To the tragic, the ironic-and-heroic sensibility, simple answers are an impossibility because they derive from wrong questions. Life consists of messes; it is the job of some to make them, that of others to clean them up. An impossible task and we do it every day. That task underlies the action of Cozzens's novels. Yet cleaning up or messing up is what the characters do and becomes the measure of the men: masters of reality, slaves of delusion, casualties of fact. To the mind imbued with a New England sense of the tragic, to a Hawthorne or a Robinson or a Cozzens, what counts is the stubbornest fact of all: life-and-death, and the two are one. Ironic, perhaps. Acceptance and the struggle to achieve it confer the heroic wisdom.

2

JOHN WILLIAM WARD

James Gould Cozzens: The Condition of Modern Man[1]

The cover of James Gould Cozzens's novel, *By Love Possessed*, bears an emblem: an old French gilt clock, precisely at the hour of three, adorned by a pastoral scene in which a cupid is about to loose his arrow at the heart of a young shepherd peeping through the vegetation at a largely undraped sleeping nymph. This clock appears in the novel, on the first and last pages, and embodies figuratively what the novel presents dramatically in the pages that lie between. *By Love Possessed,* as all of Cozzens's mature work, is about the condition of man, and in the world of James Gould Cozzens man's condition is limited. One limit is set by time, the moment in which man has his being. It is precisely three o'clock. The other limit is set by man's nature, divided between reason and passion. The shepherd is about to fall victim to the blind instincts of the heart. The burden of Cozzens's fiction is that man must recognize and accept his condition and still bear the responsibility of action. So in the final sentence of *By Love Possessed,* the hero quietly says, "I'm here." Here I am now, at this moment in all of its contingencies, not in some irrecoverable past or in some wished for future; as I am, in all my humanity, a living mixture of weakness and strength, not in some ideal state of being. To act in the full awareness of the irony of the conditions within which he must act is, for Cozzens, the dignity of man.

If this is Cozzens's theme—and it is, I think, present in all the major novels—then he may now have found his own moment in time; until now Cozzens has been neglected, but there are signs that this neglect is about to end. History has finally prepared for him an audience that can share his angle of vision. Until it did, Cozzens went his solitary way, writing fine novels, pursuing his own sense of what life is about, undeterred by the almost total absence of recognition. Beginning in 1924 with *Confusion,* a bad first novel he would like to forget, Cozzens has now written an even dozen novels. He found his major theme by the thirties and in 1948 won the Pulitzer prize with *Guard of Honor.* The *Literary History of the United States* which, as a cooperative venture in scholarship, undertook to do for our generation the definitive job on our literature, also appeared in 1948. Hardly a figure, however minor, fails to be noticed, even if only in the copious bibliography. Not a line is given James Gould Cozzens. This is not so strange as it might first seem to one who admires Cozzens. Literary fashions are not purely literary; they indicate states of mind, and the American mind was not in a state to appreciate Cozzens. It is true that Cozzens's style has had something to do with his failure to gain attention; he has none of the flair, the verbal pungency, which immediately attracts. But, of course, style and subject matter are finally one, and the fault seems to be that we were not prepared to see what the matter was. Now perhaps we can.

In *Ask Me Tomorrow,* a novel which draws closely on Cozzens's personal experience, the hero, a young writer named Francis Ellery, watches a hotel ballroom full of people and thinks that "he would have liked to write about it, if only he could grasp the dramatic inner meaning that lies in the simultaneous occurrence of diverse things." If *Ask Me Tomorrow* is somewhat autobiographical, it is so only as a portrait of the artist as a young man, because Cozzens can do what young Francis Ellery wishes he could do. The characteristic situation of Cozzens's best work is a brief and thickly-peopled moment in time in which a wide variety of characters and incidents are united by a single dramatic inner meaning. *Ask Me Tomorrow* itself covers only a few days in the life of Francis Ellery; the action of *The Last Adam* takes one month; *Men and Brethren* less than twenty-four hours; *The Just and the Unjust* begins at 10:40 on a Tuesday morning and ends just after midnight on Friday; *Guard of Honor* occupies about three days; and *By Love Possessed* precisely forty-nine hours. The strict ordering of time, the compression of action into a narrow frame, is not simply the virtuosity of a skilled storyteller, although one must admire that too. By thoroughly exploring a limited segment of human experience in all its ramifications, Cozzens means to make us appreciate more fully the complexity of moral action. Human right or wrong for Cozzens never exists outside the tangled web of time. And, as

Francis Ellery sees, diverse things happen simultaneously. A typical Cozzens novel involves a wide range of characters and a multitude of actions. The numerous subplots function together not only to intensify the dramatic inner meaning common to them all, but to show that no action takes place in isolation. Each action is irrevocably conditioned by all the others. To consider a course of action as if it were self-contained, to act as if one's will were free, is, for Cozzens, to act naïvely, to ignore the teachings of experience.

Cozzens's work is defined not only by these technical devices, the compression of dramatic time and the interpenetration of various actions, but also by certain pervading themes, the need for experience and the discrepancy between the ideal and the actual. The Cozzens hero is generally an older man or, at least, one being schooled into the wisdom of maturity. The hero of *By Love Possessed* wonders at one point if the full status of an adult is given to anyone under forty. Not by James Gould Cozzens. Colonel Ross, the old judge on wartime duty in *Guard of Honor*, puts the matter succinctly:

> Colonel Ross was not sure whether today's different attitude came from being twenty years wiser or just twenty years older. He had, of course, more knowledge of what happens in the long run, of complicated effects from simple causes, of one thing stubbornly leading to another. Experience had been busy that much longer rooting out the vestiges of youth's dear and heady hope that thistles can somehow be made to bear figs and that the end will at last justify any means that might have seemed dubious when the decision to resort to them was so wisely made. Unfortunately, when you got to your end, you found all the means to it inherent there. In short, the first exhilaration of hewing to the line waned when you had to clean up that mess of chips. The new prudence, the sagacious long-term views would save a man from many mistakes. It was a pity that the counsels of wisdom always and so obviously recommend the course to which an old man's lower spirits and failing forces inclined him anyway.

Colonel Ross's skeptical acquiescence to the stubborn facts of life is, in *Guard of Honor*, the mark of his wisdom and maturity. Cozzens measures all his heroes by the same rule. Julius Penrose, the philosophical, crippled lawyer of *By Love Possessed*, puts the code bluntly, ". . . as a wise old man once said to me: Boy, never try to piss up the wind. Principle must sometimes be shelved. Let us face the fact. In this life we cannot do everything we might like to do, nor have for ourselves everything we might like to have." But Julius Penrose points to the paradox in such a view of life. Man is not to lapse into a sullen fatalism because he cannot do all he wants to do; he must stir himself to do what he can. "The paradox is that once fact's assented to, accepted, and we stop directing our effort where effort is wasted, we usually *can* do quite a number of things, to a faint heart, impossible." To learn the art of the possible is to be mature in Cozzens's world, and it requires a long schooling in the facts of life. Colonel Ross in his novel says, "If you did not know where the limits were, how did you know that you weren't working outside them? If you were working outside them you must be working in vain." To learn where the limits are and to learn to accept them is to attain the full status of adulthood. This is present as a theme in all of Cozzens's later work, and it is at the center of one of the best, *The Just and the Unjust.*

Cozzens does a bold thing at the start of *The Just and the Unjust.* This novel is about Abner Coates, a young assistant district attorney, and the action centers largely about a trial for murder which Abner Coates helps prosecute. The novel begins at the opening of the trial in a high-ceilinged, semicircular courtroom where the acoustics give a spectator little chance of hearing anything intelligible. Abner Coates is aware that, involuntarily, he is an actor in a drama and that "his audience was finding the performance, of which he was part, a poor show compared to what true drama, the art of the theater or the motion picture, had taught them to expect. "Art would not take all day Monday to get a jury. Art never dreamed of asking its patrons to sit hour after hour over an impossible-to-hear lawyers' colloquy, with no action." Cozzens's point, of course, the point of all his novels, is that life is not dramatic; it is not filled with stirring climaxes or crucial moments. Life is the slow process of adjustment to half-seen facts and complicated decisions. Here, in *The Just and the Unjust,* he boldly invites the reader to contrast life with art. But his invitation is art. Cozzens deliberately sets himself dramatically unpromising material and then, tongue in cheek, suggests that art would never deal with such material. There is a danger here, certainly, the danger of the mimetic fallacy, to write undramatically about the undramatic. In *The Just and the Unjust* Cozzens may seem to run close to the line, but only the reader lulled into taking Cozzens at face value will miss the artful way in which *The Just and the Unjust* is put together. Although the murder trial is the subject of the book, the theme of the book is Abner's initiation into the facts of life. His love affair, his involvement in politics, the minor actions which involve a fatal automobile accident and the voyeurism of a perverted high school teacher, all work toward this single theme. *The Just and the Unjust* is a novel about the formation of a young man. Abner Coates is made to face life as it is and to accept the responsibilities of maturity, to discard his youthful protest against the distance between the way things should be and the way things are. As a quiet study of the fruits of maturity, the novel embraces a comprehensive hierarchy of ages: one of the defense attorneys is a young man in his twenties; Abner Coates is thirty-one; the district attorney is in his forties; the patient, tired and finally effective political boss is in his fifties; and Abner's father, Judge Coates, manfully bearing up under the adversity of a stroke, is in his sixties. These men represent an ascending scale of practical wisdom, so that the final words of the novel are fittingly left to Abner's elderly father. He tells his son, "We just want you to do the impossible," which is simply to get up and face life every day and do what needs to be done.

The epigraph to *The Just and the Unjust* is a quotation from Lord Hardwicke: "Certainty is the Mother of Repose; therefore the Law aims at Certainty." The novel then ironically demonstrates there can be no certainty in anything man has a hand in by dramatizing the distance between Olympian justice and its human embodiment. For Cozzens, to accept the facts of experience is to accept the discrepancy between what is and what should be; with this as a theme, he focuses his novels on those areas of modern life where the ideal is presumed to govern. The heroes of his later work are always professional men: a doctor in *The Last Adam,* a minister in *Men and Brethren,* a lawyer in *The Just and the Unjust,* a judge who doubles as a military man in *Guard of Honor,* and a lawyer again in *By Love Possessed.* Cozzens turns to the professions for his heroes because of the contrast implicit between the ideal code of the profession and the actuality which pervades it. He can measure the difference between what should be and what is most economically in those areas clearly defined by a professional standard. If, considering Cozzens as a novelist of pro-fessions, one immediately thinks of Sinclair Lewis, one must as immediately recognize a difference. Although Cozzens takes infinite care with the authentic details which command belief (Zechariah Chafee, reviewing *The Just and the Unjust* in the *Harvard Law Review,* thought it should be required reading for every young lawyer), he is not interested in the profession as such. He is sympathetic with his professional heroes because they, of all people, are aware of the discrepancy between their professions and their actions and strive, fully conscious of the irony of their predicament, to realize a goal they know is ideal.

Cozzens published his first novel while a Harvard sophomore. Later, in a dictionary of American authors, he wrote, "My first novel was written when I was nineteen, and that, and the next, and the next, were about what you would expect." Passing the same judgment on himself that he does on his characters, he said, "I have the advantage of being older now." Today, on the flyleaf of his other novels, those first novels *(Confusion, Michael Scarlett* and *Cockpit)* are never listed. Because, as Cozzens wrote a Princeton undergraduate, "I began my career with the (I know now) fantastic accident of happening on three successive publishers who lacked judgment and so accepted for publication three novels written before I had taught myself to write or had any idea of what novels should do. Most novelists of course write such first books but they remain manuscripts." One may accept Cozzens's painful sense of the inadequacy of his youthful work, yet the first, *Confusion,* strikes the very note he was to explore successfully in his mature fiction: the necessity for experience, the adjustment of the ideal to the actual. The story itself, full of preposterous Russian counts and sophomoric philosophizing, is about the defeat of innocence when exposed to the confusion of actual life. Cozzens inverts the Jamesian situation: the innocent young girl is a European, and America is the world of experience. But to think of Henry James is to weight the novel too much; its worth now is that it states at the outset the typical Cozzens situation although it fails to realize it in novelistic terms. Late in the novel, the young heroine comes to realize that life is not ideal. "There ought to be some sort of moral beauty," she says, "which isn't marred by the ridiculous or the clumsy or the inane. And you just don't find it. Each one of us has irradicable meannesses and flaws. And then things happen in such a way. Life isn't an abstract thing, it's the concrete lives of millions of human beings. When you build on life you build on a sort of quicksand."

Cozzens's developed position is an acceptance of this judgment. In Cozzens's world one does build on quicksand and one must continue to do so fully aware that he stands on shifting ground where the ideal is marred by the ridiculous and violated by the meanness of us all. Read by itself, *Confusion* might be taken as an adolescent protest that this is so; the weakness of the novel is that the reader is not sure how to take the meaning. (In *Cockpit* youth quite ingeniously triumphs over the shrewd adult world.) But by the time he had taught himself to write, Cozzens not only would avoid such infelicities as "irradicable," he would have learned how to project his own sense of life so that the reader, caught up in the fiction, must assent to its imaginative reality. No artist develops in a simple linear fashion, getting better and better, exploring his theme more deeply and more intelligently in each successive novel, but Cozzens comes close. With only slight variations from the straight line, Cozzens has steadily strengthened his grasp.

By Love Possessed is the story of forty-nine hours in the life of Arthur Winner, a tall, spare, balding, fifty-four-year-old lawyer. Early in the action, a young judge, enmeshed in his own problems, asks Arthur Winner, "Could you ever have changed what's going to happen? You know this much: Whatever happens, happens because a lot of other things have happened already. When it gets to where you come in—well, it's bound to be pretty late in the day. . . . Freedom, I read at college, is the knowledge of necessity." Arthur Winner recognizes the emotion behind the query, the dissatisfaction with the kinds of victory to be won in life. "Might all of them be forms of defeat: givings-up; compromises; assents to the second best; abandonments of hope in the face of ascertained fact that what was to be, was to be?" With a remarkable economy, every action of the book tests this question. Some characters in the novel evade the question; some escape into alcoholism or to the institutionalized comfort of the church; some lapse into a brutalized cynicism to hide from the question. But Cozzens leads the reader to an inevitable acceptance of Arthur Winner's answer at the end: "Victory is not in reaching certainties or solving mysteries; victory is in making do with uncertainties, in supporting mysteries." But if this is the answer, the conclusion is not fatalistic. Man is not excused because this is so; he cannot resign his responsibility; he cannot quit because he knows that the end of man is defeat. Stoically, using what resources of reason and strength of will he has, man must continue to seek the order which the conditions of life and man's nature will not allow. The irony is there in the hero's very name: Winner. There are no winners in Cozzens's world; the only victory is to recognize and accept that fact.

By Love Possessed was a Book-of-the-Month Club selection; Hollywood, in its fondness for the resounding sum, bought it for $100,000; *Time* magazine has even enshrined Cozzens in its pantheon of modern heroes by putting him on the cover. This sudden rush of acceptance—and one hopes that Cozzens is as immune to good fortune as to bad—raises a question. Why now? Why not before? Cozzens is aware that he has not been in fashion. Once, when invited to lecture at Princeton University on the novel, he declined, writing that he had observed "that novelists are not very interesting when they air their views about the novel. As well as grieving the judicious by glimpses they generally give of that coxcomb and jack-ass seldom far to seek in anyone with a creative faculty, those I've heard or read were never long in indicating that they don't know a damn thing about their 'art'—and that's the case, I think." In a second letter, he put emphatically his sense of his own separateness:

> Not to mince it, current critical opinion and I greatly disagree about what's good. As part of his professional job I think a novelist should examine all contemporary novels that attract attention. I do this; and I then take care to observe what critics say of them. Too often for it to be mere chance or minor difference in taste, I'm flabbergasted to find the consensus discovering Profound Feeling, Deep Insight, Moving Symbolism, and Living Characters where I saw deplorable sentimentality, cheap and childish thinking, silly pretentiousness, and preposterous people. Here, clearly, someone's wrong; and at that I'm satisfied to leave it. Like so many of those who are really self centered, absorbed altogether in what they are doing, I haven't even the weakest urge to show others their errors, argue them into agreement, prove I'm right. This makes the obvious part both of prudence and of common civility easy for me—I just shut up, stay at home, and attend to my work.

In one of the early as well as one of the few essays on Cozzens, the late Bernard De Voto, writing from the "Editor's Easy Chair" of *Harper's Magazine,* tried to answer why Cozzens had not received the critical acclaim due him; his answer may also contain the reason why acclaim has come to Cozzens now. In his usual muscular fashion, De Voto used Cozzens to cudgel modern criticism. Critics shy away from Cozzens, De Voto thought, because

> he is a writer. His novels are written. . . . So they leave criticism practically nothing to do. They are not born of a cause but of a fine novelist's feeling for the lives of people and for their destiny. . . . They contain no fog of confused thinking

on which, as on a screen, criticism can project its diagrams of meanings which the novelist did not know were there. There is in them no mass of unshaped emotion, the novelist's emotion or the characters', from which criticism can dredge up significance that becomes portentous as the critic calls our attention, and the novelist's, to it. Worse still, they are written with such justness that criticism cannot get a toe hold to tell him and us how they should have been written. Worst of all, the novelist's ego has been disciplined out of them, so criticism cannot chant its dirge about the dilemmas of the artist in our time.

Now despite much of the nonsense here, the notion that the better a writer is the less criticism has to say about him, despite this wrongheadedness, De Voto has two shrewd things to say about Cozzens's career. First, Cozzens's books are not "born of a cause"; they are not the product of any social or political movement. Second, Cozzens has not gone with the literary fashions of the time, the novel of elaborate symbolical structure, or the novel of sensitive introspection. If this is true, Cozzens has stood apart from some sizable movements in our literature. He has gone his own way which is not the way of the novel of social protest or of the psychological novel; nor has he followed the dominant mode of modern fiction, the method of symbolism.

Yet, if one goes back to the early work, one discovers that Cozzens worked successfully in the modes which now seem so alien to him. *Son of Perdition*, Cozzens's fourth novel and the one he likes to consider his real beginning, is interesting for two reasons: it marks the tentative discovery of the way Cozzens will organize his major novels while, at the same time, it wavers between two ways of handling the story. *Son of Perdition* takes place in little less than a day at Dosfuegos, Cuba, the sea terminal of the United Sugar Company. Early, then, Cozzens is working toward the tight unity he will exploit better later. Cozzens had already written one novel, *Cockpit*, about the sugar industry, but he does not make special use of his knowledge of its operations; *Son of Perdition* does not qualify as the novel of a profession. But in this early novel (although it was his fourth book, he was still only twenty-six), Cozzens is already exploring the problem of the limits of human action, the moral complexity arising from man's limitations as man. At one point in the novel Cozzens compares the clean efficiency of the machine with the muddled quality of humanity. He notes "the machine's inhuman beauty, the reason and might of the machine, confounded so inevitably by the rooted folly, the poor stubborn pride of man." But Cozzens is not arguing the program of the Italian Futurists; man's nature is not susceptible to the perfect rationality of the machine. Man is constantly the victim of his own rooted folly.

Son of Perdition has, even if as tendencies, the characteristics of Cozzens's best manner. It fails only in one, the interpenetration of the various levels of action. The novel is sharply divided between the Americans who have descended on Cuba with the United Sugar Company and the natives of Cuba. Although there is little functional relationship between them, Cozzens comes close to something brilliant in the way he juxtaposes the two societies. Two characters dominate the American group: the chief of United Sugar, Joel B. Stellow, and a drifter and troublemaker, Oliver Findley. Given their own world, they exist simply as strikingly different types. But by counter-poising them against the superstition of the natives, Cozzens surrounds Stellow and Findley with the suggestions of the symbolic roles of God and the Devil. Here Cozzens is having the best of both worlds without committing himself to either. In two subsequent novels, *S.S. San Pedro* and *Castaway*, both short books, Cozzens pursues what, for want of a more precise term, one might call the "symbolic." In actual order of chronology, *The Last Adam* falls between these two books and suggests how Cozzens was hesitantly finding his way. But before he found it, Cozzens proved he could write one of the most successful psychological novels of our contemporary fiction. *Castaway* is worlds removed from Cozzens's later work; a nightmare inversion of the Robinson Crusoe myth, it belongs to the world of Kafka. The hero, Mr. Lecky, is locked in a department store over a long weekend. With everything that modern society has to offer in the way of material goods, he is paralyzed by fear, either pursued by a madman or haunted by his own madness. Whichever, the point is clear enough: with all the material resources of the modern world, man has not the spiritual resources to sustain himself. In American literature, one must go back to Melville's "Bartleby the Scrivener," to discover another piece of fiction with the same surrealistic power. One can understand, given the critical position that Mr. De Voto bewails, that so good a critic as Stanley Edgar Hyman can think *Castaway* Cozzens's best book as well as one of the most neglected novels in recent years because Cozzens presents here, in all its psychological horror, the alienation and aloneness of modern man.

The danger, however, in drawing a sharp contrast between the stages of Cozzens's career is that one will miss in the later work the subtle way in which Cozzens has domesticated his symbolism. In *By Love Possessed,* the setting and the weather, so natural in themselves, gradually add a dimension of meaning to the novel and so, by definition, function symbolically. As the action progresses, a dark storm gathers, just as fate gradually encloses Arthur Winner. At the orgastic climax of the tender love affair between the hero and his wife, the storm breaks. The next day we learn that a bolt of lightning had at the same moment riven a great sheltering tree at Ponemah, Arthur Winner's summer house. With that news one recognizes that the idyllic security of childhood so carefully associated in the early pages of the novel with Ponemah, is not to be sustained in the adult world in which love is only fleetingly realized amidst the storms of experience. Ponemah is, in Arthur Winner's world, not only the garden of his first wife, it is *the* Garden, the world of innocence before man's fall into time and the corruption of his human estate. One need only read Cozzens's first novel, *Confusion,* in which there figures a place of retreat from the world also called Po-ne-mah, to realize what Cozzens means when he says that when he grew older he taught himself what a novel should do. It should project the world of myth and symbol in the common experience of the characters' daily lives. So when the final revelation of Arthur Winner's own character comes in a scene in the garden, the inevitable snake is believably there.

Cozzens's increasing insistence on the actual as he develops his technique is, of course, a function of his subject matter, an insistence on the here and now. So one suspects that it has never been a matter of style; it is the image of the world which the style presents and of which it is itself a part. Cozzens's central theme, that man must do what he can with the facts as they are, that one must accept the world as given, runs counter to the mood of much recent American history. Rebellion against society, which Cozzens thinks is callow, characterized the fiction of the twenties; the reformation of society, which Cozzens thinks is naïve, characterized the fiction of the thirties. Despite Bernard De Voto, Cozzens's fiction may be born of a cause, a personal cause, the cause of a skeptical conservative who does not think too much can be done with the way things are. Outside of his fiction, Cozzens has said, "I am more or less illiberal, and strongly antipathetic to all political or artistic movements. I was brought up an Episcopalian, and where I live the landed gentry are

Republican." The tone is a little shrill here, but it suggests a personal position behind the fictional world which helps one understand why Cozzens remained out of fashion despite his superior skills as a novelist. One need not be a member of the landed gentry or a Republican, of course, to appreciate Cozzens's view of the condition of man. Happily, Cozzens is a novelist, not an apologist. But it is probably true that more Americans can more readily share Cozzens's view now than ever before. Since the Second World War, high aspirations and heady ideals have come to seem somewhat embarrassing, if not a little absurd, to many Americans. So the acceptance of Cozzens today may be as much a function of the intellectual climate as was his neglect before.

If history has caught up with Cozzens, it is because, in a more important sense, history has caught up with the American people. With a remarkable prescience, Tocqueville remarked in the early nineteenth century that because of the social conditions of the country Americans "owe nothing to any man; they expect nothing from any man; they acquire the habit of always considering themselves as standing alone, and they are apt to imagine that their whole destiny is in their own hands." The cast of mind Tocqueville perceived led on one side to the Horatio Alger legend and the myth of the self-made man in the hands of the apologists for our great capitalists. On the other, it led to great literature and the creation of a characteristic American hero, the solitary, self-propellant man, heroically alone. He is the character demanded by Emerson and given us most richly by Thoreau in *Walden,* the new man who realizes his character by taking his way not to man but from man. Since 1783 when Crevecoeur asked his famous question, "What is this new man, this American?" down to Henry James's hero Christopher Newman, named after the discoverer who gave this new man a new world in which to act, Americans have tended to think of themselves as beginning history over again, making a fresh new start. The westering experience of the American people dramatized in their daily lives the notion that the archetypal American was he who moved away from society, out of civilization, and began anew. He is Natty Bumppo and Huck Finn. R. W. B. Lewis has explored with brilliance the cultural dialogue that took place around and about the heroic figure and has named him the American Adam.

The image of the American as a new man was not without its paradoxes, of course, and Hawthorne and Melville have alerted us to them. But the chief irony in such a dramatization of American history was that the moral Nature of the Transcendentalists and the Jeffersonians was also the physical one of coal, iron and oil, the raw materials of a vast complex industrial civilization in which man's direction is to man, not away from man. Henry Adams made this irony the central fact in *The Education* and saw that "the new American [was] the child of incalculable coal-power, chemical power, electric power, and radiating energy." Emerson could innocently write that history was but the lengthened shadow of a man, but when Adams returned from England to the new industrial America that had won the Civil War he "found his energies exhausted in the effort to see his own length. The new Americans, of whom he was to be one, must, whether they were fit or unfit, create a world of their own," but it was to be the world we now live in, the world of complex structures, interdependence and organization, not the world of freedom from social forces and escape from history.

Richard Blackmur once said in conversation that James Gould Cozzens was the only contemporary writer who had taken the organization of modern society for his theme. Because Cozzens does not write about the man in the gray flannel suit many readers will miss the fact that Cozzens is a contemporary writer in the deepest sense of the term. His subject is the limited world in which man is enmeshed in a congeries of forces which radiates far beyond his personal control. Cozzens's heroes are professional men, themselves an instance of a specialized society, and his subjects are various; but his theme is the complex world in which man, in his already limited estate, is further limited. In *Guard of Honor,* seemingly about the special state of war, Cozzens asks if war is really so different: "No. Not if you could face the too-little-faced fact that war really brought you nothing that peace, mere living, couldn't eventually bring." Mere living can be a heroic enterprise in Cozzens's fiction because it involves man in a historical and social web that he can neither control nor renounce. All he can do is the impossible, live in it and accept it with skeptical and ironic good sense.

Henry Adams wrote that the "old-fashioned logical drama required unity and sense; the actual drama is a pointless puzzle, without even an intrigue." Adams is describing the modern world; Cozzens's heroes live in it. The point is not that Cozzens may have read Adams (although their mutual admiration of Pascal suggests an intellectual affinity) but that both are reacting imaginatively to the conditions of modern man. The view of human nature present in Cozzens's fiction is not modern; it has roots certainly in the seventeenth century, echoes of which sound throughout Cozzens's pages. But it is a view of man, however traditional, which has a special significance for modern man. Divided between reason and passion, called to act in a world he cannot control, he may be the new man, the new hero, that the conditions of modern life demand. If so, James Gould Cozzens has presented him richly for our contemplation.

3

PIERRE MICHEL

Cozzens and the
Conservative Spirit

Although he began publishing novels in 1924, at the age of twenty-onc, James Gould Cozzens received little recognition from the public and the critics until the 1940s and 50s. His early novels and many of his stories (most appeared in the 1920s and 30s) have now, with the author's approval, sunk into oblivion; Cozzens regards them as juvenile and clumsy, and his publisher does not even list them any more. He received the Pulitzer Prize for *Guard of Honor* (1948), his best work and one of the most technically accomplished novels of the 1940s. *By Love Possessed,* his next novel (1957), which won the Howells Medal of the American Academy of Arts and Letters in 1960, became, almost overnight, as the *Morning Noon and Night* blurb stated, "one of the notable best sellers in contemporary fiction"; indeed, it caused an uproar whose echoes reverberated throughout the country and even abroad. It was hailed as a masterpiece, praised as the novel of the decade, and one critic nominated Cozzens for the Nobel Prize. Others, piqued by the political or philosophical views they perceived in Cozzens's fiction, accused him of all possible sins, literary and other. Much of what was said was grossly exaggerated. After the tumult over *By Love Possessed* had subsided, critics returned to a less excited appraisal of Cozzens's work. The *succès de scandale* of *By Love Possessed* was the occasion for many to take stock of Cozzens's other productions and to discover a novelist who did not claim to propose spectacular solutions for the evils of the world, who put forward his views in a quiet, unobtrusive way and with a subdued tone, and whose style and sense of structure were often brilliant.

The question naturally arises as to why *By Love Possessed* caused so much more of an uproar than did *Guard of Honor*, a superior novel, or even *The Just and the Unjust*. It seems probable that many upper-middle-class white Anglo-Saxon Protestants could easily identify, perhaps with some envy, with the novel's "aristocrats," with their self-righteousness and what could be interpreted as their antiminority feelings. Look, the reasoning would go, how badly those inferior people regularly fumble things, and, on the other hand, with how much fortitude we bear our hardships. Though this may not be exactly Cozzens's point, this is certainly how the novel could be interpreted, and has been.

Besides, it seems that at the time *By Love Possessed* was received by critics more as a philosophico-political event than as a merely literary one. John William Ward has argued that it fitted the intellectual atmosphere of the fifties: "Cozzens's fiction may be born of . . . the cause of a skeptical conservative who does not think too much can be done with the way things are. . . . it is probably true that more Americans can more readily share Cozzens's view now than ever before. Since the Second World War, high aspirations and heady ideals have come to seem somewhat embarrassing . . . to many Americans. So the acceptance of Cozzens today may be as much a function of the intellectual climate as was his neglect before."[1] Leo Marx disagreed with Ward's implication that Cozzens's vogue was a measure of the American people's new maturity; Marx rather saw in it something "akin to the apathy and moral resignation" of the Eisenhower era that seems to sanction a regression, a dangerous withdrawal from the realities of historical change.[2] Contrary to the 1960s, not many questions were asked openly in the 50s; the big issues that came to an explosive foreground in the following decade were still in limbo, and the characters of *By Love Possessed* dismiss them rather expeditiously or approach them with the utmost timidity. One cannot help perceiving a splendid irony in the coincidental publication of *By Love Possessed,* a book which, if anything, tended to comfort a large section of the American public in its self-satisfaction and adherence to the status quo, and the launching of the first Sputnik, an event that contributed much to awakening America from its post–World War II somnolence.

Cozzens stands outside the well-trodden paths of contemporary American fiction; he has shied away from the themes of alienation, rebellion, dissent, and protest that have proliferated in American literature of this century and more particularly in the post–World

War II period. Technical experimentation and the techniques of the absurdists and of black humorists are even more remote from his preoccupations. He is infrequently mentioned by critics, and when he is, it is only in passing in surveys of American literature since 1945. More strangely, he is seldom ranked among his contemporaries, those writers born around the turn of the century or in the first decade of the twentieth century. Yet many of them have not been able to produce fiction so consistently concerned with man's fundamental fears, worries, and joys, and with the life of human communities in Northeastern America. But in his better fiction, which extends from *S.S. San Pedro* (1931) to *By Love Possessed* (1957),[3] Cozzens assumes an attitude, tackles material, and expounds a number of views that may be called conservative and that, to be sure, are regarded by many not only as outdated but also as very unpopular. Cozzens may indeed represent only a minority view; he does not dabble in the spectacular, nor does he in any way attempt to ride the moment's fashion. If it is true that his single-mindedness and his concentration on certain themes alien to the mood of the 60s and 70s may have repelled many critics and readers, we should not forget that what he has to say is perfectly legitimate and is sustained by a high aesthetic achievement.

Tony Tanner, in his *The Reign of Wonder*[4] remarks that few major American writers have actually taken their material from society; among the great formative works of the American imagination, he cites *Huck Finn,* which is set on a river, *Song of Myself,* on an open road, *Moby-Dick* on the sea, and *Walden,* by a pond. Even though *The Scarlet Letter* confronts some of the complexities engendered by the relationship between nature and society, the central figure in the novel is Hester, alienated in the forest. In support of his observation, Tanner cites Tocqueville's remark that "each citizen is habitually engaged in the contemplation of a very puny object, namely himself," and if he looks away from the self he sees only "the immense form of society at large or the still more imposing aspect of mankind. . . . What lies between is a void." Between the particular (the individual) and the general (mankind) lies society, man's proper environment. Tanner concludes, somewhat regretfully, that society is often ignored in American literature and too frequently broken down in "minutely scrutinized particulars" which lead to "large and often vague affirmative generalizations."[5] And Tanner adds that American literature "has often shown an inability to move beyond one particular syndrome of responses—wonder keeling over into horror, delight switching to disillusion, revulsion locked with awe. It has shown itself, perhaps, too suspicious of the analytical intellect, too disinclined to develop a complex reaction to society, too much given to extreme reactions, too hungry for metaphysics."[6] Echoing Tanner, the *Times Literary Supplement* of 25 November 1965 stated that "the deepest privacies in American life, the radical detachments, are those of nervous breakdown, of addiction, of protracted silence."

Cozzens, on the contrary, takes a close look at the various elements of society, which he regards as an organism with its own complexity and intricacy; since it is man's natural environment, he tells us, how it functions and how man behaves in its midst is worth analyzing in detail, and he chooses his settings not just for their isolation and all-inclusiveness but also for the opportunity they offer him to examine the social hierarchy, the patterns of power, and the ways in which social elements of all sorts interact. As early a novel as *S. S. San Pedro* (1931) offers a good case in point. No community could be more self-enclosed than the crew and the passengers of a ship; though their association as a community is only temporary, it has a life of its own. It is clear that Cozzens is already interested in the flow of power, the chain of command without which, as he convincingly demonstrates when it breaks down, any community would lose its protective function and its structure would simply collapse. Cozzens holds on to the same approach in his novels after *S. S. San Pedro* (with the exception of *Ask Me Tomorrow*). His main interest lies in the life of those small communities he selects, especially in times of crises. In addition, he picks one member of that community from whose point of view he tells the story; that particular social organism is therefore examined from within, and its tensions and antagonisms appear all the more clearly and convincingly.

Society is not seen from a distance, nor as an enemy, not even as a necessary evil with which one has to seek accommodation; nor is it ever shown as oppressing or corrupting man, but as protecting him, a view seldom propounded in contemporary literature, to be sure. Left to himself, man would not be the sacred animal, the demigod he is often made out to be by Cozzens's confrères in literature. Nor is Cozzens in the least concerned with the various forms of metaphysical anguish so popular nowadays. He is very careful not to deal with situations that might give rise to such preoccupations or, if he does, these preoccupations are not allowed to develop beyond the socially useful. Even though in *Men and Brethren* Ernest Cudlipp may have grave doubts about his faith and the dogmas of his Church, and even though he suffers a serious spiritual crisis, he realizes that he is only a small piece in a complicated mosaic and does not engage in metaphysical considerations and discard all responsibility. Most of Cozzens's main characters, after all, would have good reasons to drop everything and run away; contrary to their peers in contemporary fiction, however, they turn back to society, to the existing patterns, for protection for themselves and, in turn, for others.

Cozzens becomes increasingly impatient with the reformers, ideologists, and defenders of causes and utopias who appear regularly in his novels, especially *Guard of Honor* and *Men and Brethren,* because he does not believe in the existence of a superior truth that would determine the course of history. He does not embark on a crusade, or on a quest, as in *Moby-Dick,* or on a search for universal love, as in Salinger. The reader should not expect to find in his fiction any metaphysical or ideological interpretations of society—except for those which Cozzens presents sarcastically. Such futile preoccupations, he implies, can be indulged in only by those who have performed the impossible task of settling all the problems of everyday life in a specific community.

Cozzens's fiction is grounded in the here and now, in the concrete and palpable. His characters do not withdraw. They do not lose themselves in the anonymity and strangeness of metropolises or in the social vacuum of the desert or the road; they surround themselves with the familiar, the community (sometimes even the social class), the small town, the army base. These locales all have sharp limits in Cozzens's novels: the ship *(S.S. San Pedro),* the small New England *(The Last Adam)* or Eastern Pennsylvania town *(The Just and the Unjust* and *By Love Possessed),* the New York parish *(Men and Brethren),* the Army base *(Guard of Honor).* Even *Castaway* is worth mentioning here, for, though it is one of those few Cozzens novels that have nothing to do with his "conservatism," its action takes place solely within the confines of a department store and its only character is utterly isolated in it. Yet the set-up of *Castaway* is, in all other respects, atypical of the rest of Cozzens's fiction. Cozzens packs his communities with large numbers of characters and institutions, all of which interact in a complex web of relationships. Referring to *Guard of Honor,* Cozzens once wrote: "I wanted to show that real (as I now saw it) meaning of the whole business, the peculiar effects of the inter-action of innumerable individuals functioning in ways at once determined by and determining the functioning of innumerable others—all in the common and in every case nearly helpless involvement in what had ceased to be just an 'organization' . . . and became if not an organism with life and purposes of its own, at least an entity, like a crowd."[7] But it is not just the wealth of material that gives life to his communities; his characters, varied and different as they are, are never stereotyped because they are all inserted into contexts teeming with life.

The intruding world outside, especially in *The Just and the Unjust, Guard of Honor,* and *By Love Possessed,* always represents an actual or potential danger to the proper functioning of the community. Cozzens's aristocrats resent any interference, not only because it may threaten the stability of the community but also because it might endanger their own power in it, in which case such intrusions sometimes reveal prejudices or preconceptions in Cozzens's characters. Some of the "responsible citizens" in *The Last Adam* and *By Love Possessed* lose a good deal of their aura because of such prejudices, which they not only harbor but also express. It is clear that Cozzens's intention, in an effort to avoid sanctifying his Rosses and Winners, is to give his reader a balanced picture of these characters and to show that everything has to be taken with a grain of salt. Whether he is successful in all cases will be discussed later.

It is symptomatic, too, that social, religious, or political changes and reforms are in nearly all cases put forth by outsiders or people with little experience in the matter at hand. In *The Last Adam* new, more sophisticated medical techniques belong in another town and do not prove to be any more effective than Dr. Bull's old country medicine. The directives concerning racial integration in *Guard of Honor* come from Washington and are judged by Colonel Ross to be inapplicable to Ocanara Air Base. Such examples, all generative of incidents, abound in Cozzens's novels and accurately reflect the conservative spirit (or the spirit of preservation) that prevails in the small, self-enclosed communities toward which Cozzens shows a predilection. Change and reform, when they must take place, must be initiated from within. If George Bull in *The Last Adam,* Ernest Cudlipp in *Men and Brethren,* Martin Bunting in *The Just and the Unjust,* and Arthur Winner in *By Love Possessed* could erect around their communities the kind of fence that surrounds Ocanara Air Base they certainly would—although to some extent the fence proves ineffective.

Furthermore it is significant that, with one exception *(Guard of Honor),* Cozzens has chosen settings in the older part of the country, towns to whose history of order, stability, "unchangeableness" he often refers, which all have twentieth-century equivalents of the colonial common in the courthouse, the church (even in *Men and Brethren,* set in New York City), and the town meeting-hall *(The Last Adam).* Not only do those places have an identity of their own, but they force some identity upon their members: one cannot be anonymous in a small town; identification—positive or negative— with the community is inevitable. On the one hand, the attachment of many of Cozzens's characters to their immediate environments (the town, the old houses) is emotional, indicating that they seek and find psychological and moral security in the past and feel insecure about what lies ahead. But it is just as clear that, heeding Burke's remark that "I put my foot in the track of our forefathers, where I can neither wander nor stumble," they regard whatever is inherited from the past, or is established by history (the Eastern small town), or by experience (the law), or by reverence (the church) as worth respecting and preserving. This traditional viewpoint is illustrated by the enormous difference in the treatment of the church between *By Love Possessed* and *Men and Brethren.*

For one thing, the characters in *By Love Possessed* resent Roman Catholicism as an intrusion, as a religious form brought in by non-WASP Americans, and as authoritarian and vulgar. In *Men and Brethren,* the Episcopal Church is subjected to other pressures, those of the big city. The parishioners seem to have lost all sense of identification with it and the church remains in the background, although the novel's central character is one of its ministers. In the twenty-four hours that the novel covers, Cudlipp does not even set foot in the church. He is hardly concerned with service, doctrine, and dogma, as if the weight of the big city had rendered such activities and preoccupations, if not impossible, at least irrelevant, and had turned the church into a sort of center for ethical counseling and social work. We are given exactly the opposite picture in *By Love Possessed;* here the church, far away from the megalopolis and protected from change by the "responsible" people in Brocton, remains a place of worship.

Cozzens takes a mixed view of man. Nowhere do his "admirable" characters, his "aristoi," express the belief that human nature is innately depraved and corrupted, but they all agree that it is highly unreliable; their conservatism in this matter is neither a throwback to John Adams, for whom all men were bad by nature, not to Jefferson, whose optimism they would deride. Cozzens stresses repeatedly in his mature novels man's strong propensity to be taken in by emotions and lust *(By Love Possessed),* illusions, theories, causes, utopias *(Men and Brethren, The Just and the Unjust, Guard of Honor);* even reason *(By Love Possessed)* is shown to be unable to solve everything because human intellectual and mental capacities are limited. Not that the "aristoi" refuse to see the validity of theories and utopias *in vacuo,* or that they do not acknowledge the existence of good intentions; there is nothing Ernest Cudlipp or Colonel Ross can object to in the charitable intentions of Wilber Quinn or Jim Edsell; these two young men are merely trying to correct social wrongs. What irks Cudlipp and Ross in their ineptitude or lack of realism and the havoc they are apt to wreak if unchecked. They would agree with Burke that "however pure the intentions of their authors may have been, we all know that the event has been unfortunate." Burke's further remark that "the question is, not whether their spirit deserves praise or blame, but—what, in the name of God, shall we do with it?" is the kind of question that often comes to Colonel Ross's mind in *Guard of Honor* or Arthur Winner's in *By Love Possessed.*

Interestingly enough, Cozzens manages to inject some irony in the situations he creates: many of his "aristoi" are shown to commit the same sins as those defenders of causes and utopias they scorn. Too much reliance on man's rationality, Abner Coates and Arthur Winner learn, also can lead to disasters, for it can conceal from them a certain reality made largely of precisely what is irrational in man. These characters are, in a way, punished for their arrogance. But at the same time, and this is what distinguishes them fundamentally from their fellow sinners referred to above, they are "redeemable," for they are aware of their failings and therefore try to adjust, while the defenders of causes persist in their errors.

A prudent man, Cozzens offers no panacea for man's failings, nor any universal solution for the moral, psychological, or other difficulties that assail him. In several of his novels, he stages situations which point to the way human nature can be held in check. In *By Love Possessed,* Ralph Detweiler's stupidities must be stopped, not just because they are silly, but because they are harmful to others; if necessary the law may even be called upon to stop him. In *The Just and the Unjust* the criminals are dealt the punishment they deserve, even though the ending of the book is fraught with an irony that neatly sums up Cozzens's tongue-in-cheek view of man's reason and unreason: the jury, whose function it is to safeguard society's rights in the enforcement of the law, allows itself to be swayed by the defense counsel's spurious arguments, spurns the letter of the law and turns against society's interest. But as Judge Coates, the novel's wise commentator, adds, what is cannot be changed or ignored: the only way out of a difficulty is to seek accommodation with the actual, with the way things are, a view Colonel Ross shares and stresses repeatedly in *Guard of Honor*. It is vain and childish to wish things were different. The pragmatic test comes first. What, Cudlipp asks himself in *Men and Brethren,* are we to do with Geraldine Binney, a married woman who has deserted her husband and whom her lover has made pregnant? Society's and the church's positions are clear-cut, but in Cudlipp's view they would solve only half the problem; they would, at any rate, rule out the solution Cudlipp advocates and implements: an abortion. He places himself in the wrong with the law and with the church but manages to handle the situation with the fewest possible harmful consequences.

But another kind of limitation confronts Cozzens's realists, although it evolves significantly from *S.S. San Pedro* to *By Love Possessed*. In *S.S. San Pedro* and *The Last Adam* the sense of the inexplicability of events, of "an indifference so colossal, so utterly indifferent," is stressed strongly and repeatedly. Man is placed in situations from which he is given no chance at all to escape; much occurs in which logical explanations of the course of events are beyond his intelligence. The ship and its crew in *S.S. San Pedro* and the sick in *The Last Adam* are helpless playthings of fate and their survival depends on the whims of circumstances. In the later novels, man is allowed a choice within certain limits. Cudlipp may elect to help Mrs. Binney (and the assistance he can offer may assume a variety of forms), or he may refuse to see her; Abner Coates, Colonel Ross, Arthur Winner are constantly faced with the necessity of making choices. Of course those choices must always be made within the narrow limits set by circumstances, with the result that these men can only choose between alternatives that do not particularly appeal to them and which, were they left entirely free, they would not even consider. In an explicit passage in *By Love Possessed*, Arthur Winner, prompted by a friend's opinion that "Whatever happens, happens because a lot of other things have happened already,"[8] views his first wife's life and death as a continuous succession of "caused effect after caused effect to effective cause after effective cause."

This sense of man's limitations should not be taken for a deeply pessimistic feeling that nothing can be done. Obviously, Cozzens's intention is not to describe man as an inadequate, aimless, meaningless biological accident, irrevocably crushed in the vise of metaphysical determinism. Cozzens display none of the social determinism of a Farrell, none of the "chemical determinism" of a Dreiser, and none of the racial determinism of a Wright; nor are his characters driven, like new Chillingworths or Ahabs, by a pathological psychic condition to clash against the normal course of life. The deep pessimism often associated with the notion of determinism in literature is absent from his novels. Caught in a chain of inextricably linked events, the individual's free will is limited, but neither Cozzens nor his heroes seem to despair over it. They are expected to do what they can with what little they are given.

It is society, with its various obligations and institutions, which operates as the most reliable and most experienced restraint on man's unruly nature. Cozzens's society is a society of inequalities, natural as well as artificial, as is exemplified in the military hierarchical pattern of *Guard of Honor*. Not decried as unjust, as it is in much of contemporary fiction, the chain of order and command appears as the pattern that holds the community together, for it is shaken and endangered once one of its links fails. The point is made splendidly in the first part of *Guard of Honor*, one of Cozzens's best passages. It opens on a scene of beauty, calm, peace, and, perhaps more importantly, of order, discipline, and respect for rules and regulations. Full harmony is maintained until one person disobeys instructions and bedlam follows. Equality, many of Cozzens's "aristoi" would hold *(The Just and the Unjust)*, would inevitably lead to the rule of the mob, hence disorder and anarchy, while inequality, in a democracy at least, would ensure, if not total, certainly greater freedom than anarchy.

This stand should not surprise the reader, since Cozzens gives only the point of view of the top members of his small town or military communities. When observed from this vantage point, the social configuration is given a particular twist; Cozzens's view is exclusively a view from the top, that of the professional upper-middle-class, doctors, ministers, high-ranking officers, lawyers, judges, people whose interest is not to alter the pattern of a society which has made it possible for them to rise so high, and, in most cases, whose professional duty it is to keep society functioning. This is precisely what makes them political conservatives at heart. We have already mentioned their abhorrence of outside interference. They profess, more or less openly, the same reluctance to accept change from within. This is why, among other things, the grievances of people less fortunate are frequently derided, their claims deemed unjustified, their errors perhaps a little too often attributed to their social or intellectual inferiority.

Many readers will grow nervous with Cozzens here. That his men at the top are providentially the best can be attributed to the fact that they have risen because they are top-notch; yet some readers may feel that there is so much virtue, honesty, intelligence, foresight, or sheer luck in Cozzens's leaders that the dice seem to be loaded in their favor. They are all WASPs with latent prejudices against hyphenated Americans or members of the minorities, or simply those less fortunate than they are. Ross may regard with dismay the interracial tension on the base and may regret that such hatred exists in his country; yet for all his regrets, such difficulties may persist at large so long as they do not disturb the microcosm he has to administer.

On the other hand, Cozzens's leaders are "aristoi" with a sense of duty that often goes much beyond that of mere service. *Noblesse oblige* is what prompts Abner Coates, Ernest Cudlipp, Colonel Ross, and Arthur Winner to take into their hands the destiny of their community, or a fragment of it, beyond professional duty. The argument is that, did they not do so, a disaster of sorts would be bound to ensue. That his gentry of talent and virtue occasionally proves fallible is a point which Cozzens is careful to make, often with irony *(The Just and the Unjust, By Love Possessed)*.

Central in Cozzens's work, especially in the later novels, is the question of man's rights and duties. He takes great pains to show that in the kind of society that appears in his fiction, man's rights are fully protected; the criminals in *The Just and the Unjust* do not get off scot-free, but they are dealt with much less severely than was originally expected and they get a chance to exercise their rights to a full extent. The notion of due process of law, which operates as a protection for the individual, is paramount in the minds of all the responsible characters in this novel, just as it is in Arthur Winner's mind when he agrees to assume Ralph Detweiler's defense. But those criminals and Ralph Detweiler are in turn guilty of having harmed others, i.e., of having neglected their fundamental duty in society. For if he is protected by the law, man is, in turn, expected to show due respect for the interests and the good of others.

This is undoubtedly a relatively narrow definition of the notion of duty; man's duty to an abstraction (the nation, religion, or a cause) is hardly ever mentioned, and when it is, it is apt to be frowned upon (see Edsell in *Guard of Honor*) or even derided (Wilber Quinn in *Men and Brethren*). To lofty ideals or aspirations, Cozzens's responsible character clearly prefers a pragmatic definition of his duty in society: very often, it simply boils down to the necessity for picking up the pieces *(Guard of Honor)* or carrying on what others have begun, even though it may be illegal *(By Love Possessed)*, the overriding concern being that order should be maintained and that the existing state of affairs should not be disrupted. Arthur Winner decides to sacrifice his own integrity, though only in his own eyes, not publicly, because being honest—i.e., in this case, feeling good—would send people to jail and ruin others. He prefers to keep silent, though he knows it will give him a bad conscience. Winner comes down from his lofty pedestal just as, in *Men and Brethren,* Cudlipp abandons his plans to introduce a few innovations into the activities of his parish; his duty, his superior reminds him, is to avoid rocking the boat, and Cudlipp finds himself later in the ironic position of having to admonish his assistant for the same reason and picking up the pieces after him. Again, Colonel Ross's justification for assuming command of the Army Base is simply that everybody seems to have forfeited his responsibilities and the chain of command would be in danger of collapsing if someone did not take over.

But one's judgment must be tempered. If Cozzens opposes change and reforms *per se,* he does not turn his "aristoi" into standpatters who would resist evolution even when it proves to be necessary. Changes in racial relationships do take place in *By Love Possessed,* and the novel's "aristoi" accept them willingly, although they are not above voicing some prejudices occasionally. The best illustration of cautious change occurs in *Guard of Honor,* in which Ross has to adapt Washington's liberal directives to local conditions. He resents federal intrusion into local affairs as potentially productive of unchecked and unadapted, hence dangerous, change. He regards those directives and the egalitarian principles of Jim Edsell and his friends with the same mistrust. At the same time, he has to curb the racial aggressiveness of a number of Southerners on the base. Again the pragmatic test comes first: Ross steers a cautious course, makes changes because he wants to avoid trouble, and introduces those reforms that are precisely least likely to make any further stir. He is, like all of Cozzens's other responsible characters, a realist; to that extent, he is admirable. But, some readers would object, the question is whether he would introduce those changes if trouble were not brewing; it does not seem to have occurred to him that blacks were treated unfairly on the base until someone pointed it out to him.

The two institutions—the law and the church—around which Cozzens organizes his communities are by nature generative of order, stability, and continuity. The law is presented, especially in *The Just and the Unjust,* as the product of a long experiment, a compound of forces slowly, carefully, and deliberately amassed, hence an institution which, because of its wisdom, past and present, and its stabilizing effect on society, ought not to be tinkered with. As Arthur Winner puts it in *By Love Possessed:* "This science, as inexact as medicine, must do its justice with the imprecision of wisdom, the pragmatism of a long, a mighty experience." In any case, as *The Just and the Unjust* shows very clearly, it must be protected from the corrupting influence of human emotions; Cozzens, writing in 1951, seems to have been echoing Judge Coates, his "wise commentator" in *The Just and the Unjust:* "If it [the law] has a single fault or flaw, I lay that to the unfortunate intrusion of the human element—a fallibility and unreasonableness of mankind that enters to disturb the law's own august order of right and reason."[9] The law is far from perfect— because it is man-made—and the legal machinery can sometimes be defeated by the very guarantees society has built into it *(The Just and the Unjust).* There are hints that it could be improved but only after due deliberation and with extreme caution.

It is revealing that in *The Just and the Unjust, Guard of Honor,* and *By Love Possessed,* the main characters are all men of law, as if the legal profession were, for Cozzens, a privileged vantage point from which to observe society. Another reason why Cozzens is so strongly inter- ested in the things of the law is that they provide him and his "aristoi" with a relatively rigid pattern, generative of order, for the study of society. Much of what he sees outside it is chaos, as exemplified by what happens when people disregard the law *(The Just and the Unjust and By Love Possessed),* or stand outside a pattern that can be assimi- lated to law: military regulations in *Guard of Honor.*

The church, also a product of the past, fulfills essentially the same function; not only is it the guardian of morality and thus sets moral standards for man, it also encourages him to behave according to set norms of ceremony and formality. It remains the venerable mother of all Christians; its role remains fundamentally moral and spiritual, not social (a charitable institution, as it tends to be depicted a little ironically in *Men and Brethren*), not as a place to which man may turn when he feels the "need to belong," as a sort of surrogate for what

society can no longer offer. In *By Love Possessed,* the church adds
another dimension to society, that of formality, tradition, respect,
but it is viewed as only one of those segments which altogether form
the whole of society. The Episcopal Church is presented repeatedly
as an American institution because of the democratic spirit which
pervades its structure and hierarchy and its acceptance of the separation of church and state. The non-respect of these two fundamental principles is what allows Arthur Winner and Julius Penrose
in *By Love Possessed* to criticize the Roman Catholic Church, whose
intransigent attitude they regard as a threat to some of America's
most cherished institutions.

Cozzens's novels address themselves to the observation of social
realities and the formulation, or suggestion, of moral comment.
They concern themselves with society and the individual's relationship to it. Their vision may be narrow in that the locales are limited
geographically, the choice of characters, socially speaking, is consistently the same, the philosophical and political angle of attack are
similar throughout.

If Cozzens belongs to those novelists who "record," who accept
society as it exists and are primarily concerned with presenting it as
such, he still does not remain uncommitted; his conservative stance
involves him just as much as rebellion, or despair, or alienation
involve other writers. His acceptance of the social order, that "complex reticulation of institutions and individuals which, with all its
imperfections, stands against the barbarous condition of anarchy,"[10]
is not just grist for his mill but his very subject.

If indeed Cozzens's "aristoi" want to conserve, they prefer to do so
discriminately and intelligently. Shunning realities of modern life
such as the mercantile spirit of business or the helter-skelter of
megalopolises, they retreat to small towns, small enough communities to remain organic though complex, supervised by "aristocrats" who have a strong sense of service and duty and whose main
concern is the survival of that organism in the midst of a generally
hostile outside world. That such communities may be doomed to
disappear and be replaced by other collectivities where the individual's role is necessarily submerged in the achievements of the collectivity (the corporation, the law firm, the hospital, the university) does
not seem to bother them. They do not, after all, look to the future
but prefer to build the present on the known and stable foundations
of the past.

That particular view of life to which Cozzens and his characters are committed makes them "rooted" conservatives rather than "rootless" ones. Indeed, they stand closer to Edmund Burke or, in twentieth-century terms, to New Conservatives like Russell Kirk, than to "adjusted" conservatives like Clinton Rossiter, or to the radical right, or to old-guard Republicans.[11] Their conservatism is fraught with a preoccupation with man and society which brings them very close to what Paul Elmer More and Irving Babbitt termed "new humanism."

Many will see in Cozzens's fiction only a resurgence of the attitudes and mannerisms of the Genteel Tradition. His increasing propensity to use "fine" style, with its sometimes overcomplex sentences and its plethora of latinate words[12] points to his conviction that language is not just a means of communication but a part of man's heritage that is meant to be cherished and cultivated. But if Cozzens prefers to retreat to a certain gentility, if he chooses to ignore the upheavals—political, spiritual, and psychological—of our world, he does give us a view that, after all, has just as much merit: he offers a careful consideration of man living in the companionship of his fellows.

4

ROBERT SCHOLES

Moral Realism:
The Development of an Attitude[1]

The following quotations may be read as a dialogue. The first
speaker is a young man in a novel of 1929. The second is an old man
in a novel of 1942.

> That was what you did. You died. You did not know what it
> was about. You never had time to learn. They threw you in
> and told you the rules and the first time they caught you off
> base they killed you. Or they killed you gratuitously like
> Aymo. Or gave you the syphilis like Rinaldi. But they
> killed you in the end. You could count on that. Stay around
> and they would kill you.

> Don't be cynical. . . . A cynic is just a man who found out when
> he was about ten that there wasn't any Santa Claus, and he's
> still upset. Yet, there'll be more war; and soon, I don't doubt.
> There always has been. There'll be deaths and disappoint-
> ments and failures. When they come, you meet them. Nobody
> promises you a good time or an easy time. I don't know who it
> was who said when we think of the past we regret and when
> we think of the future we fear. And with reason. But no bets
> are off. There is the present to think of, and as long as you live
> there always will be.[2]

The young man who spoke first was Frederic Henry in Ernest
Hemingway's *A Farewell to Arms;* the old man who answered was
Judge Coates in James Gould Cozzens's *The Just and the Unjust.* I do

not wish to suggest that Cozzens in this passage is consciously and specifically attempting to rebut Hemingway. Rather, my intention in juxtaposing the two is to locate the unknown by its relation to the known—to make Cozzens's view of life clear by its polar opposition to the more familiar vision of the cosmos characteristic of Hemingway.

His view of life is certainly the right place to begin a consideration of James Gould Cozzens as a writer of fiction. This is true for a number of reasons. First, he is much more than most American writers of his generation a novelist of ideas. Second, and possibly because of the first reason, his technical development as a literary artist has been intimately connected with the development of his thought. This is not to say that he uses fiction (like George Orwell, for example) as a vehicle for polemical thought, but that a particular and very carefully worked-out attitude toward life operates in his fiction to determine the essentials of plot, character, and setting.

The speech of old Judge Coates from the end of *The Just and the Unjust* is characteristic enough to stand as a fair statement of the attitude toward life that dominates Cozzens's later and best fiction. But it is only characteristic. It is not an ultimate formulation, a solution to the problems of living. It represents a significant phase in his thinking, which is associated with much of his best work, but it represents a phase only—not the whole process of thought. The process is the important thing—the continuing development that began with his earliest fiction and is still in progress.

The early novels are *Confusion* (1924), *Michael Scarlett* (1925), *Cock Pit* (1928), and *The Son of Perdition* (1929). Cozzens was an undergraduate at Harvard when his first book was published—an event he has since regretted;

> It made me, in my own eyes, a real figure in literature, at once; an author of far too much promise to waste time any longer at schoolboy work. So I quit school and got at my career, started right in at what I thought was the top. In that way every natural fault was solidified, and it is taking all my effort now, in my mid-thirties, to wipe out those faults, to really learn to write.[3]

This separation of the first four novels from the later works is not entirely a device of criticism on my part. Indeed, they were first dissociated by their author, who has failed to mention any of them in the lists of "Other Books by James Gould Cozzens" that appear opposite the title pages of his later works. That his repudiation of his earliest works is a result of their technical shortcomings can certainly be inferred from his statement just quoted, but there is yet another reason why at that time he found these early novels "much too painful to talk about."

> When I was that age I admired a friend of mine who got drunk at 9 o'clock in the morning. That is too early in life to begin to think of yourself as a writer. Because you are very young when you think a fellow who comes to your rooms early in the morning, already drunk, and is heaving bottles against near-by walls at noon, is entirely admirable.[4]

The reasons for the repudiation of these first four novels were more than technical. In fact, the implication seems to be that it is the greenness of judgment rather than the technical faults which makes those first books "much too painful to talk about."

Confusion is a novel about a girl who develops a sensibility too exquisite to allow her to function in a world that has too little to offer her. In the matter of theme the book bears a close resemblance to a work published in the following year: *The Great Gatsby* by F. Scott Fitzgerald. Gatsby is described as having "something gorgeous about him, some heightened sensitivity to the promises of life, as if he were related to one of those intricate machines that register earthquakes ten thousand miles away." Cerise D'Atrée, the heroine of *Confusion,* has something of this same "heightened sensitivity to the promises of life." The descendant of an ancient French family, Cerise is given the best education the resources of her family and the intelligence of her two godfathers can provide. As she grows up, these two well-meaning gentlemen become aware that something has gone wrong. The more sensitive of the two, Tischoifsky, expresses it in this way:

> We gave her the past in full measure, we laid a foundation of exquisite sensibility and appreciation. It was to have been her most ready servant. It has turned on her and she is going to be its slave. You can see it. She has a remarkable instinctive taste in things. She has a youthful capacity for idealization, of course. Ordinarily the realization of life as it is—to use that for lack of a better phrase—would fall on semi-developed taste and immature appreciation. Both those safeguards we have obliterated in Cerise, we have put years and constant effort into obliterating. Now you see Cerise stripped of all

protection except the unreliable slowness of experience to divulge the full force of disappointment.[5]

Later the disenchanted bride, Jacqueline Atkinson, directly tells Cerise essentially the same thing about herself: ". . . I'd hate to see it happen to you. And you're one of the ones it would happen to. You're looking for more in life than there is . . ." (p. 327). The death of Cerise in an automobile accident is meant, I am sure, to emphasize the world's inability to fulfill her, as well as to bring the story to a conclusion.

Fitzgerald and Cozzens in these two books both seem to feel that there is something wrong with a world that can not present such people as Gatsby and Cerise with "something commensurate to their capacity for wonder." The difference between the two novels—aside from any question of superiority of technique—is that *The Great Gatsby* is ripe Fitzgerald, while *Confusion* is very green Cozzens.

This motif of a sensitive young person destroyed by an indifferently cruel world is repeated in Cozzens's second book, *Michael Scarlett*. This is a historical novel, set in Elizabethan England, in which such characters as Nashe, Marlowe, Donne, Shakespeare, Southampton, and Essex figure prominently. But for all its period setting, the main outline of the story is very like that of Cerise D'Atrée. Michael Scarlett is "an exquisite youth" raised by a guardian, educated but sheltered—just as Cerise was. He comes as a young man into a Cambridge and a London alive with faction and is soon unwittingly embroiled. Shakespeare and Southampton speak of him:

> "I would have thought," commented Mr. Shakespere, "that my lord Essex, Mr. Marlowe, and Mr. Nashe between them dominated him wholly; they call, and he comes. A strange melancholy of indecision hath smitten you young people, Harry. Him chiefest of all."
>
> "I had not meant to hint I liked him less," answered Southampton quickly, "but that I pitied him more. It was an evil thing he ever came to London. See how an unplanned, undesired chain of event hath placed him in the saddle where he sits neither safe nor happy. Essex was fitted to taste in his championing of the high party. Essex requires aid at a duel (by irony, on Michael's behalf). Michael, with nice swordsmanship, saves the day and Devereux's life; yet so greviously hurting Captain Blunt that he transfers the popu-

lar leadership of his party from Essex to himself, which he
neither wanted nor needed, and having, can neither manage
nor hold. He doth not understand the issue, he cares little for
the outcome. Those that do care, borrow his name to forward
their own ends. Being confused and not comprehending, he
hath submitted thus far."[6]

Michael's death results from a senseless fight in which he attempts to
enable Nashe, wanted for an accidental killing, to escape capture.
Nashe refuses to flee, but fights by Michael's side until wounded.

In the last chapter of *Confusion*, "White Roses," the dying Cerise
had gazed from her bed at a vase full of roses and mused that it was
"strange that a rose which would presently die should be so beautiful" (p. 401). A rose figures in the closing pages of *Michael Scarlett*,
too. Michael, bleeding to death in the snow, asks a mad prostitute to
deliver to Southampton a memento he has carried in his shirt. He
dies as she removes the object and inspects it.

> "How, a rose?" she murmured, "i' faith, a pretty wooden
> rose, yet much decayed and dry."
> She tossed it up and down as a child tosses a toy.
> "Poor rose, sweet rose," she sang, "yet thou'rt very dead."
> She looked at it for a space.
> "Prithee burn, rose," she said.
> It fell into the fire and was lost. (p. 318)

In each novel the roses, living or dead, seem to represent (clumsily,
perhaps) the young person whose life and death has been the matter
of the story. The suggestion that life is a sad affair because beautiful
roses and exquisite young people must die in its confusion can only
be described as sentimental. It is undoubtedly this sentimentalism,
strikingly evident in the early novels, that makes their author so
reluctant to discuss them.

It seems for a time in the third novel, *Cock Pit* (1928), that the
familiar pattern of the first two is to be repeated. The story is set in
Cuba against the prominent background of the sugar industry. The
principal focus is on the daughter of an engineer at one of the mills.

Ruth Micks is not an "exquisite youth" as Cerise D'Atrée and
Michael Scarlett were, but she is superior to and in conflict with her
environment. The discerning bank manager, Mr. Britton, observes
and judges her:

> He took a swallow of wine. Romanticists! His own practical

mind made allowances for it as one would make allowances for the difficulties of a cripple.

That cool and calculating efficiency of thought and judgment which made him one of the bank's most trusted managers appraised ... them all. ... He had othing but admiration for Ruth, unlikely to criticize an intelligence which he felt to be understandable, like his own. Across it ran the softer stuff, the gentler, yes, stupider, sentiments of Mary and Maurice. Ruth went through them like steel through wax.

No; he held that. Not steel. You missed Ruth altogether if you could see only that clean cutting power. That was superficial, a clear head working easily among muddled ones. His own clear head could recognize that with admiration, but there was something deeper, he knew, for he felt, totally unsentimental, an attachment for Ruth, a sense of understanding her, of seeing what none of these people saw, not even her father. His mind with a clearing flash, like the dropping of the jumbled pieces of a kaleidoscope into perfect pattern, held it there.

By God, he thought, not surprised, for he had known it all along, he supposed; what a rotten shame! *Not even her father. . . .*

An unutterable and very simple sadness came over him. It turned from Ruth, for that was the end he saw, not temporary, but a final frustration.[7]

There is a hint in Britton's meditation, which occurs midway through the novel, that Ruth's story is to end in frustration as Michael's and Cerise's had, but it remains only a hint, ultimately belied by the plot. At the close of the story Ruth is a successful heroine, having conquered by her cleverness and courage the ruthless sugar baron, Don Miguel Bautizo. Don Miguel is not only defeated, he is made to like it, demonstrating that under his ruthless exterior beats the heart of a gallant gentleman.

The musings of Britton serve to illustrate a conflict that will prove most important for an understanding of Cozzens's novels. His opening condemnation of "romanticists" sounds a theme that recurs with increasing emphasis in Cozzens's work. The qualities Britton marks in those "romanticists" are "stupider sentiments" and "muddled" heads, which are opposed to the "understandable" intelligences and "clear" heads of Ruth and himself. Since it is Ruth's clear head that prevails in the novel, we may assume that the author shares to some extent in Britton's condemnation of romanticists. Yet the state of affairs pictured at the end of the story is clearly the result of a sentimental or romantic way of looking at life. To believe that a young woman may triumph over the armed rapaciousness of a large and powerful industry is surely the result of a sentimental conception of reality; and to believe that the unprincipled head of such an enterprise, a man who once quashed the report of a United States Senate Committee, is likely to turn out to be a cavalier old gentleman is even more romantic.

In this way a novel has been produced that specifically attacks muddled thinking and sentiment under the name of "romanticism" but which can be shown to be vulnerable to the same charges in regard to its plot and at least one of its characterizations. This then is the sort of book a young man who thinks that "a fellow who comes to your rooms early in the morning, already drunk, . . . is entirely admirable," might be expected to write. And this is the sort of book that a middle-aged man, who no longer finds such antics entirely admirable, might be expected to find it "painful" to have written.

Still the struggle between sense and sensibility was clearly joined in this novel, and, if the victory of sense was marred because it was achieved in a sentimental manner, there were to be other struggles. In the works of the eight years following the publication of *Cock Pit* in 1928, this conflict was renewed again and again. The vague anti-romantic notions that began to take shape in *Cock Pit* were gradually formulated into a complete and consistent doctrine, most explicitly expounded in *Men and Brethren* (1936); and, finally, this doctrine has been qualified and enriched in the later works.

The Son of Perdition (1929), like *Cock Pit,* is a product of Cozzens's year in Cuba, but despite the similarity in setting, it is a very different book from its predecessor. It represents a considerable advance in technique: an attempt, perhaps not quite successful, to do more than was done in the early novels. And we can observe in it an important shift in thematic emphasis.

Cozzens's first three novels dealt with the efforts of young people to adjust to their environments. The exquisite youths, Cerise and Michael, perished without succeeding. The clear-headed Ruth triumphed, but in a sentimental way. The central conflict in *The Son of Perdition* occurs within a mature man. Joel Stellow is the Administrator General of the United Sugar Company, a post that gives him a truly despotic power. The company has its own railroads, its own banks, its own armed guards, even its own villages. Stellow chooses to exercise his power benevolently—insofar as this is compatible with the best interests of the United Sugar Company. And herein lies the central conflict of the novel.

The particular crisis that exposes this conflict is brought about by the arrival in Stellow's little kingdom of a dissolute American, Oliver Findley. Wherever Findley is, there is trouble. In part this is caused by his personal characteristics. He is a liar, a thief, and a drunkard; and these facets of his character cause their share of difficulties. But beyond this, there is something about him that seems to act as a catalyst, bringing into violent action the potential danger or evil latent in any given situation. He strolls into a sugar mill; a man is crushed in the machinery. He asks a bartender to drink with him; the man's boss enters and fires the bartender for drinking on duty. He seduces a Cuban girl; a whole complex of terrible intrafamily emotions, hitherto balanced against one another, are unbalanced, resulting in a murder. From the most serious to the almost trivial, trouble follows in the wake of Oliver Findley. He is thought to be the Devil by Pepe Rijo, the simple mayor of the United Sugar village of Dosfuegos. His relation to Stellow is adumbrated by the book's epigraph:

> —those that thou gavest me I have kept, and none of them is lost, but the son of perdition.—*St. John* 17:12.

Findley, of course, is the son of perdition; Stellow the man who tries to keep "those that thou gavest me."

When Findley turns up at a United mill, General Administrator Stellow tries to find a use for him. A ticket to Habana and fifty dollars are to be his reward for a little chore. Leaving Stellow's office, Findley appraises the great man:

> He wasn't sure, as he went out, that he understood Mr. Stellow—the man, that was, apart from the Administrator, the individual in contradistinction to the United Sugar Company. It was probably a shift from one to the other; from the Company, which asked what could be done with a liar and a thief, to the individual who tried to find a use in the face of that absolute nothing. A curious unemotional sympathy which would wish, for reasons too hard to guess, to give a human being a break where it was possible without hamper-

ing the Company. He wondered, struck by the thought, if Mr. Stellow, after these many years, had reached a point where he needed to believe that a human being could hamper the Company.[8]

Stellow soon finds that Oliver Findley is not a man who can be given "a break." The son of perdition is caught stealing the same day. The Administrator, feeling that Habana is not far enough, decides to ship his guest to Bordeaux:

> "I don't believe you'll ever get back to Cuba again," he said. "That's all I care about, Findley. Wherever you go there'll be trouble, and it's not going to be here. It's too late to make you over, Findley."
>
> A change close to expression had moved Mr. Stellow's face; nothing direct, like pity or indignation. Only a trace of a sag, a contraction of the gray eyes. . . . Oliver Findley stood dumbly in the shadows, even his own relief lost in this final astonishment.
>
> For the first time he saw Mr. Stellow as a person. He saw him in the ultimate, incredible obviousness of a human being apart from his position, divested of the small excrescences of habit and particular personality. Mr. Stellow was old, simply, and tired; as all men must be sooner or later. In the Administrator's last words had been also his own epitaph, and all his life, all that the eye had seen and the brain considered, could serve him no better than to make him understand it. (pp. 144–45)

Findley is shipped off to Dosfuegos for further shipment to France. In the short space of time before he boards the ship he is the cause of an incident that affects Stellow not merely in his capacity as Administrator, but personally.

One of Joel Stellow's few friends, perhaps his only one, has been Vidal Monaga. Monaga is a fisherman, but because of his monumental family pride he is able to meet the Administrator as an equal. Findley casually seduces Nida Monaga, the daughter of Vidal. Nida's brother Osmundo suspects this seduction, and in his attack on Findley reveals to his father that his own relations with his sister are not purely brotherly. The old man, out of pride in his name, murders his son. He is imprisoned by the major of the village until Stellow can get there. On arrival the Administrator asks him to explain why he did it. Vidal explains that recent events have shown him that his son, now a grown man, did not know what it was to be a Monaga; and "Being sure of this, I saw that he would be better dead" (p. 248). Stellow, whose power is unlimited, has a report of accidental death prepared by his doctor. This effort to save his old friend from trial is frustrated by the man's pride in himself. Their conversation is overheard by Findley:

> "You are released from the Alcalde's order of arrest," said Mr. Stellow. "The matter is officially closed."
>
> It had never, reflected Oliver Findley, been open. Never in Mr. Stellow's mind, could it have been possible to allow the mechanical processes to grind up the simple stone of this old man. It went farther than that, no doubt. The wordless bond silently and invisibly held them too close. Such destruction would break down something of Mr. Stellow. Some saving faith.
>
> Oliver Findley thought of it, seeing clearly now, moved more than he would have thought possible. He saw too, the transparent farce of it. Mr. Stellow setting up himself against himself. Driving the mills and railroads on one hand, covering the face of the machines with the fiction of this necessary illusion on the other, sustaining futilely the legend of man and his dignity and freedom, long after the last remnants were dust under the revolving wheels. . . .
>
> In the electric lighted room Vidal Monaga said, "No señor. . . . That I could not do. . . . It is not much to be a Monaga to any one but me, señor. But I will be turned over to the authorities, please. . . . Because of justice. . . ."
>
> Finally Mr. Stellow answered: "As you wish." (pp. 302–3)

To Findley, Monaga's refusal to avoid justice represents a victory for man over the machine: "the machine's inhuman beauty, the reason and might of the machine, confounded so inevitably by the rooted folly, the poor stubborn pride of man" (p. 304).

One of the major faults of the book lies in the difficulties presented by having as its central intelligence a character so depraved as Oliver Findley. How much weight can we put on such a summing up of action as that quoted above? To attribute to such a dissolute wretch the clear insight needed to judge others is an error on the part of the author, equivalent to attributing a gentlemanly soul to a rapacious sugar baron. To rely on such a character to sum up, in the closing lines of a book, the action just culminated, is a technical error stemming from the sentimental error.

Another difficulty in the novel lies in its somewhat disordered complexity. There are numerous minor actions and characters, most of which seem to belong to the plot rather than the theme, and which tend to blur the theme, making the need for clarification of it especially vital. That we are forced to rely on Findley for such clarification thus assumes even greater importance than it might in a better-ordered novel.

The significance of *The Son of Perdition* in the development of Cozzens's ethical attitude is that it represents a progress from the preoccupation with the problems of youth toward the less purely self-centered problems of mature individuals. The struggle within Stellow, between his duty to the company and his care for humanity—though sketched rather than developed in this novel—is a struggle that is more central in life than are the youthful flutterings of the early novels. But the book fails—aside from the technical difficulties—to give a moral order to the struggle presented. Other than a vague preference for people over machines, there seems to be present no unifying moral attitude. Is the triumph of humanity over the machine, acclaimed by Findley, punishment for Joel Stellow or vindication of him? Is Stellow's phrase of acquiescence to Monaga's desire—"As you wish"—the speech of a man who sees a higher truth than his own, or that of a man who has lost "some saving faith?"

This fuzziness of theme persists in the work of Cozzens for some years. His next works attempt by various devices to get around the problem of ethical attitude rather than to solve the problem by taking a stand. This is particularly noticeable in the two short novels, *S.S. San Pedro* (1931) and *Castaway* (1934).

It is probably best to consider these two short works together even though the full-length novel, *The Last Adam* (1933), was published before *Castaway*. These two novellas are experiments that have not been repeated, though they exhibit excellently some abilities and characteristics of their author. *The Last Adam,* however, is in the main stream of his development, where it appears as a marked advance over *The Son of Perdition* in the direction of the major novels.

S.S. San Pedro was first published as a prize-winning story in *Scribner's Magazine* in August of 1930. It is a fictionalized reconstruction of the actual events in the sinking of the S.S. *Vestris* in November 1928. The real disaster captured the journalistic imagination in its day because of some mysterious circumstances connected with the sinking. The ship left Hoboken bound for Brazil. She ran into heavy seas almost immediately, took on a list, and struggled ahead with cargo shifting and water entering the ship, probably through the submerged coal ports. The circumstance that disturbed the public so greatly was that the ship apparently had been in this state for a day and a night without sending out an SOS. A theory advanced was that the captain "seems to have been more afraid of salvage than he was of death."[9] The ship sank with considerable loss of life. Cozzens, working from the "transcript of the hearing before the U.S. Commissioner in New York,"[10] set about reconstructing one way in which such a disaster might occur. The events are seen through the eyes of the second officer, Anthony Bradell, and the Brazilian first quartermaster, Miro. The officer and the man, each extremely capable at his job, are unable to prevent the disaster. They can do nothing to avoid the ultimate, because of the structure of command, which requires action to be initiated at the top. Captain Clendening is overcome by a strange lethargy that renders him incapable of the necessary action. That this may happen is foreshadowed early in the book by the captain's doctor, who takes Bradell aside before going ashore and warns him about the captain's health:

> "The captain," he said very low to Anthony, "is an old man, Mr. Bradell."
> "What did you say, sir?" asked Anthony, taken aback.
> "People grow old, Mr. Bradell. They break down, they wear out."[11]

Dr. Percival, who gives Bradell this warning, has a face like a death's head:

> Doctor Percival's tight face was fleshless and almost gray. His lips sank in, rounded over his teeth. They were lips so scanty that you could see the line of the teeth meeting. His eyes, red-rimmed, lay limp in their sockets, appearing to have no color at all. Doctor Percival's intense pale gaze came out of holes covered with soft, semitransparent lenses. His head, one observed, jolted, was utterly hairless, and a pale-reddish star, a mark like a healed wound, lay across the crown. Every modulation of bone showed through a sere leaf of old skin. (p. 11)

It is this face that Bradell sees at his side as he lies injured at the feet of Miro while the ship is about to founder. The story is told in a

dispassionate "documentary" style, combining graphic observation
of the physical details of the ship with the rather labored symbolism
of the death-doctor. We are given an excruciatingly careful description of a foreordained event; thus no moral issues are raised. By
choosing to depict the captain as the victim of forces beyond any
man's control, Cozzens avoids the moral questions that might be
raised had he made the problem the obvious one of the captain's
weighing salvage costs against the possibility of weathering the
storm. The whole of the action is carefully removed from the moral
world of ethical choices.

    Castaway is a story in many ways differnt from all of Cozzens's
work, but bearing a closer resemblance to *S.S. San Pedro* than to any
of his other books. It is the story of Mr. Lecky, cast away, not on a
desert island but in a deserted department store. The epigraph is
from *Robinson Crusoe*:

> . . . how infinitely good that Providence is, which has provided
> in its government of mankind such narrow bounds to his sight
> and knowledge of things; and though he walks in the midst
> of so many thousand dangers, the sight of which if discovered
> to him, would distract his mind and sink his spirits, he is kept
> serene and calm by having the events of things hid from
> his eyes. . . .

This epigraph is—like others of Cozzens's—an ironic one. It is
precisely Lecky's fear of unseen dangers that destroys any possibility
of his leading a peaceful existence in the great store. He is certain
that there is someone else in the building: "the idiot" as Lecky calls
him. Armed with a shotgun from the sporting goods department
and a knife from kitchenware, he hunts the idiot down and kills him
brutally. Then he discovers whom he has killed.

> Crouching as he turned up the fearful face, he bent his own
> face toward it, saw it again. His hand on the head, studying
> the uninjured side, Mr. Lecky beheld its familiar strange-
> ness—not like a stranger's face, and yet it was no friend's face,
> nor the face of anyone he had ever met.
>   What this could mean held him, bent closer, questioning in
> the gloom; and suddenly his hand let go . . . for Mr. Lecky
> knew why he had never seen a man with this face. He knew
> who had been pursued and cruelly killed, who was now dead
> and would never climb more stairs. He knew why Mr. Lecky
> could never have for his own the stock of this great store.[12]

Presumably he has killed himself. One critic assures us that this is an allegory that "translates readily into half-a-dozen frames of reference (centering around a ritual of rebirth)."[13] If one can believe that Lecky is a "God-Figure," and the idiot a "Devil-Figure" in a "dubious battle long ago joined," then perhaps their struggle has some large moral applications, but I find this conclusion as doubtful as the premises, which are very dubious indeed.

The descriptions of the store are as meticulous as those of the ship in *S.S. San Pedro,* and the inevitable action proceeds to its conclusion under the same uncommitted camera-eye. But this refusal on the part of the author to commit himself to a moral position could not be maintained in all his works. For, as Henry James said of Dickens, "a novelist very soon has need of a little philosophy. . . . When he comes to tell the story of a passion . . . he becomes a moralist as well as an artist. He must know *man* as well as *men,* and to know man is to be a philosopher."[14]

Cozzens's philosophy, which seemed rather fuzzy in *The Son of Perdition* (1929), was to appear in unmistakable clarity in *Men and Brethren* (1936). In an effort to isolate some of the elements that compose that clarified attitude, I will consider some of the short stories published between 1930 and 1938.

These twenty-one stories tend to divide into three groups. The largest group, comprising almost half of the stories, is composed of potboilers.[15] The second group all deal with the same subject, a boys' preparatory school. The third group includes stories interesting primarily for the light they throw on themes treated at greater length in the novels. The groups can not be dealt with chronologically, for each of them covers nearly the entire span over which Cozzens wrote short stories. There is little that can be said about the potboilers, except to note that they get increasingly slick from first to last; but the prep school stories are significant in that they deal with young people in a way quite different from the treatment of exquisite youths in the early novels. The school in the stories, Durham, is unquestionably modeled on the Kent School in Connecticut at which Cozzens prepared for Harvard. It is relevant to note at this time that Cozzens's first published work appeared in the pages of the *Atlantic Monthly* while he was in the fourth form at Kent.

The occasion of this event was an article by Edward Parmalee in the January 1920 issue of the *Atlantic Monthly* that expressed disapproval of the boarding-school system, making the charge that rigid discipline stifled any impulses the boys might have to learn self-government, and asking the question, "would not better results be obtained by a less autocratic and a more democratic system of government?"[16]

Young Cozzens's reply, entitled "A Democratic School," made the point that institutions such as Parmalee was calling for did, indeed, exist and were successful. The prefect system, under which discipline was administered by three members of the sixth form appointed by the headmaster, and two members each from the fifth and fourth forms, elected by their peers, was a truly democratic system, he maintained, and added, "Perhaps it does n't sound practicable, but then, it works." Note the emphasis on the practical and the present: "I will . . . offer the solution—not the visionary solution, but the solution that, in one school at least, works to-day."[17] The young man who wrote the article on "A Democratic School" in 1920 seems in certain ways closer to the older man who wrote the Durham stories and the later novels than to the author of *Confusion,* which appeared only four years after the magazine article.

There are five Durham stories, the earliest appearing in 1930, the last in 1938. The only character who appears in more than one is the headmaster, Dr. Holt. The headmaster is an eminently practical man who understands equally well rebellious young people and demanding parents. The student and the school, as the individual and society in microcosm, provide a type of conflict that stimulates Cozzens to an extremely revealing series of comments on rebellious idealists in general.

"Some Day You'll Be Sorry" (*Saturday Evening Post,* 21 June 1930) is about a boy who nurtures a grudge against the headmaster. The boy's rebellion is based in part on some rather stimulating reading: "Smith III, as the saying goes, had read a book. It was Paine's *Age of Reason.*" The following observation on Smith by Cozzens is interesting for the generalization it leads to: "Smith III's intelligence was much too acute to waste its strength in a permanent and ridiculous war with his environment. Real rebels are rarely anything but second rate outside their rebellion; the drain of time and temper is ruinous to any other accomplishment."

"Some Day You'll Be Sorry" is an especially interesting story because of its autobiographical overtones. As Frederick Bracher pointed out some years ago, youth versus age is a major theme in Cozzens's work.[18] Now as bits of biographical information begin to become accessible, it is apparent that one of the favorite pastimes of the elder Cozzens has been chastising the recollected figure of his youth.

> When, early in his fourth-form year, Smith III took occasion to inform the headmaster that he no longer believed in God, Doctor Holt sighed. Smith III's point had been that he did not see how he could honorably go to chapel when he considered the practice a superstitious farce. It is usual to hear most about the other side of these things—Shelley, at Oxford, is almost unbearably familiar—so it is worth a moment to consider Doctor Holt's position, confronted by a supercilious and impudent youth who appeared to get the only exercise he took from making trouble; who was very justly suspected of smoking without permission; whose marks were bad, and whose comments on life, society and the school were fitted nicely to the puerile sensation they made. (p. 47)

Smith III seems almost certainly to represent the way in which his own youth appeared to the very clear gaze of the maturing James Gould Cozzens in 1930.

A rather more mature rebel is presented in "Guns of the Enemy" (*Saturday Evening Post*, 1 Nov. 1930). This is a very fine story in which World War I descends on Durham in the form of a French officer. The ensuing conflict—among the agitated students, a young pacifist instructor, and Dr. Holt who sees the war as a monster that will destroy the youth to whom he is devoting his life—is endowed with a significance somewhat larger than that of a minor uprising in a small boys' school. "War was already enhanced by a noble solemnity and an emotional importance. Our attitude was, in fact, exactly that of America; with the special local result that when we took things hard, less than usual was said about it. When little is said, much must be taken for granted. As you know, what people took for granted was that we were fighting for humanity and could no longer allow the Germans to infest the earth" (p. 74). Dr. Holt does not share this attitude. He clearly sees the war as a horror, but he "had the courage—and courage it is if you value your reputation as a thoughtful man—to state: 'Our country, right or wrong.' Most people mistake the statement for jingoism, but it can be—and in Doctor Holt's case it was—the hard, honorable answer to an intolerable question" (p. 74). The man whose attitude disrupts the school is the young teacher, Mr. Van Artevelde. His pacifist leanings provoke a senseless physical assault from a student, whom Dr. Holt is then forced to expel. The school is threatened by a mass resignation in protest against the expulsion, but Dr. Holt, by main force of personality and skill in handling his boys, prevents this. Van Artevelde

> was, naturally, a socialist of some sort. In those years directly before the war, almost everyone who had the happiness to be young, intelligent and carefully educated was a socialist. This was in part simple intellectual snobbery, and the first cold wind from the world as it was blew it away, but Van was also an idealist, as well as being stubborn. To men of his temper, socialism's pathetic impracticality is not its worst argument; just as the principal charm of pacifism may be its dangerous unpopularity. (p. 77)

Durham figures only in the background for "Total Stranger" (*Saturday Evening Post,* 15 February 1936), another fine story, which won the O. Henry Prize. A boy is being driven back to school by his father, who is the object of a grumpy, misunderstanding rebellion on the part of the son. The father "could see no sense in breaking the simple, necessary rules of any organized society; and wasting time was worse than wrong, it was mad and dissolute. Time lost, he very well knew, can never be recovered."

The boy feels this way: "In my position, I supposed that he would always do his lessons, never break any rules, and probably end up a prefect, with his rowing colors and a football letter—in fact, with everything that I would like, if only the first steps toward them did not seem so dull and difficult. Since they did, I was confirmed in my impression that it was impossible to please him. Since it was impossible, I had long been resolved not to care whether I pleased him or not. Practice had made not caring fairly easy" (p. 8). On the trip an incident occurs that makes the son realize that his father was young once—is a human being. He begins to see that his father's is not an impossible goal reached by a perfect human being: "Unfortunately, I never did do much better at school. But that year and the years following, I would occasionally try to, for I thought it would please my father" (p. 100).

The last Durham story, "Son and Heir," (*Saturday Evening Post,* 2 April 1938), is about another rebellious boy. This boy, an excellent hockey player, is embarrassed by his father's desire to push him. He tries to take out his resentment against his father and the school (the father is Durham '09) by disgracing Durham in a hockey game—not by playing badly, but by acting in an unsportsmanlike manner. Dr. Holt, in a locker room chat, helps him to grow up a little. The author comments: "Having no intent or volition of its own, he might guess that the world—surely it is the sum of a young man's possible education—would pay out to him, not with malice and not with pity, the things that were his" (p. 91).

The view of life implicit and explicit in these stories is consistent throughout. It is the classic conservative view. The father who "could see no sense in breaking the simple necessary rules of any organized society" is pictured as a good man and a not unreasonable one. Dr. Holt, whose principal occupation in the stories is the conservative one of trying to hold together his little world in the face of disruptive influences, is presented sympathetically. The rebels are given short shrift. The name that persistently comes to mind as one reads these stories is Edmund Burke. The positive side: the organic conception of society; and the negative side: the fierce distrust and suspicion of rebels in general are both present. The particular hostility to the influence of Thomas Paine is characteristic of both Burke and Cozzens. Thus a reference to Paine in Cozzens's 1940 interview should not come as a surprise to us.

> This Summer I intend to spend many pleasant mornings hanging around court rooms because I plan to write a novel about a lawyer. "The Summer Soldier" probably will be the title. When Paine used that phrase he disdained the people who could be so described, he was calling on the men of his generation to forget their own concerns and fight for the ideal of the Revolution, to lose themselves in an ideal. He had no use for the militiamen who were willing to fight when they could afford the time, but wanted to spend most of the year raising crops, attending to business, taking care of their families.
>
> But as I see it there is a lot to be said for these Summer soldiers. The idealist, the intellectuals, haven't done any too well by the world.[19]

The attitude so clearly present in the short stories as early as 1930 is reaffirmed in this interview of 1940, and has remained an important factor in all Cozzens's later novels. The ethical attitude developed from the vague sentimentality of his earliest works through the various negations of what he calls "romanticism," "sentimentalism," and "idealism" to a firm position Cozzens calls simply "realism," and to which I have added the qualifying adjective, *moral,* to prevent any confusion of this ethical attitude with the literary or esthetic doctrine of realism. It was the development of this ethical attitude that enabled James Gould Cozzens to produce the works we now recognize as major.

5

COLIN S. CASS

The Title of *The Last Adam*

Since 1933, James Gould Cozzens's novel, *The Last Adam,*[1] has received a considerable amount of published criticism. Pierre Michel's *Checklist*[2] cites seventy sources, including fifteen reviews and one article on *The Last Adam* alone. The five books about Cozzens naturally discuss it, and many scholarly articles and later reviews mention it. Nevertheless, the author's fundamental intentions have thus far gone unrecognized, the surest indication being that his title remains unexplicated. The book's artistry and profundity have, as a result, been underestimated.

Interpretation of the title is complicated somewhat in that the English edition is known as *A Cure of Flesh.* Richard M. Ludwig reports that "Cozzens preferred *Bodies Terrestrial* or *A Cure of Flesh* to *The Last Adam;* Alfred Harcourt did not."[3] In a letter to me, Cozzens refers to his English title: "The fact: yes, my title was *Bodies Terrestrial,* for Harcourt, put in place of *a Cure of Flesh* used in fact by Longmans in England where to [sic] correlation to *A Cure of Souls* was intelligible."[4]

The latter allusion is to a phrase in Thomas Hood's "Ode to Rae Wilson, Esq." Hood, replying to Rae Wilson's published strictures on Hood's "profaneness and ribaldry," writes a variously humorous and trenchant poem attacking sanctimonious censors. As for himself, Hood agrees that

> I'm not a saint.
> Not one of these self-constituted saints,
> Quacks—not physicians—in the cure of souls,

Censors who sniff out mortal taints,
And call the devil over his own coals—
Those pseudo Privy Councillors of God,
Who write down judgments with a pen hard-nibb'd . . .
Yet sure of heav'n themselves, as if they'd cribb'd
Th' impression of St. Peter's keys in wax![5]

The resemblance of Hood's position to George Bull's is obvious. Just as Hood is no self-constituted saint in the cure of souls, so Bull is no saint in the cure of flesh. Like the poem, the novel cultivates the contrasts between the accused Dr. Bull and his superficially more saintly rival, Dr. Verney, as well as Bull's sanctimonious critics in the town, mainly to the discomfiture of the latter.

As for *Bodies Terrestrial,* it comes verbatim from I Corinthians 15:40, only five verses from the phrase, "the last Adam." It thus confirms the inference that I Corinthians 15:45 is the true source of the American title, as, indeed, did Cozzens himself. Shown an early draft of this article, he answered that "Scripture reference is of course correct. . . ."[6] It is well to have "A Cure of Flesh" and "Bodies Terrestrial" accounted for, particularly since there prove to be no interpretive inconsistencies among the three titles. Yet "The Last Adam" is the title that illuminates the author's intentions with especial clarity.

The first reviewers found *The Last Adam* likable and commendably realistic, yet shallow.[7] The similarity among their opinions suggests two things: that the book is superficially convincing, which is true; and subtle enough to be repeatedly mistaken for a shallow work— slick, miscellaneous, non-serious, lacking in scope and depth—when it is nothing of the kind. Time has not deepened our knowledge much. Critics do refer glibly to George Bull's Adamic this and that, but only two scholars—Frederick Bracher[8] and R. W. Lewis[9]—have seriously considered the title, with inconclusive results. In short, *The Last Adam* deserves a closer reading. The truth is that beneath its readable and impeccably realistic surface, it is a richly allusive response to the two greatest religious myths of western civilization.

The title is from I Corinthians 15:45, but a reader who did not recognize the allusion would think first of Adam in Eden, and the novel would reward him. George Bull's rattlesnake hunt, for instance, alludes bluntly to Genesis. Attacking the first snake, George stamps "his hob-nailed heel on it" (p. 162). To kill another, he leaps, "both nailed boots and his better than two hundred pounds landing on her" (p. 162). Cozzens plainly refers to Genesis 3:15: "And I will put enmity between thee [the serpent] and the woman, and between thy seed and her seed; it shall bruise thy head, and thou shalt bruise his heel." Once, Bull shouts, " 'Here's one son of Satan who'll never see town!' " (p. 163). Critics, though noticing these signs, have never followed them down to the subliteral reaches of a complicated book. Even R. W. Lewis, the best analyst, after calling the snake hunt "interestingly allusive," objects that it is also "somewhat intrusive," being "a mere decorative addition to the plot."[10]

Cozzens probably hoped that readers, alerted by the title and the snake hunt, would recognize his more subtle Edenic allusions. For instance, that "a universal mist went off the earth" (p. 127) echoes Genesis 2:6, the verse immediately before the creation of Adam:

> 6 But there went up a mist from the earth, and watered the whole face of the ground.
> 7 And the Lord God formed man of the dust of the ground, and breathed into his nostrils the breath of life; and man became a living soul.

Unobtrusively, the Edenic motif includes Janet Cardmaker, Bull's mistress. Just as Eve was not to eat from the tree (Gen. 2:17), so Janet had been "expected to order her life on the accepted lines of a dreary, drily educated, consciously high-thinking, virtue" (p. 36). Instead, Janet seduced George Bull, much the way Eve tempted Adam. Janet took the initiative: " 'This is my room. Come in a minute' " (p. 36), whereas George "was sure that the idea of seducing Janet had never entered" his head (p. 36). When she serves George the hard cider, and when she later "looked past the barn and the bare apple trees" (p. 177), Cozzens may allude to the forbidden fruit. He probably remembers also that after the Fall, the Lord made "coats of skins, and clothed them" (Gen. 3:21), for when George visits Janet he wears a "swinging fur" coat, and she wears "a garment which she had made herself—eight or ten red fox skins sewed over an old cloth coat" and a "round cap, also of fox skin" (p. 32).

The Last Adam follows Genesis in broader outlines, too. Of the many episodes that disturb Bull's peace, one begins by interrupting his sleep and ends in the death of Sal Peters in childbirth. It looks extraneous, unrelated to the typhoid epidemic. Yet it is consistent with the Edenic motif, since Eve's punishment was that "I will greatly mutiply thy sorrow and thy conception; in sorrow thou shalt bring forth children . . ." (Gen. 3:16). The episode agrees with its Old

Testament text, first by showing that "Pregnancy was a woman's hard luck" (p. 245); second, by introducing Sal's sister-in-law, Betty, who can sympathize "because of her own long history of sexual miseries" (p. 245), not in childbirth, but with men in a tobacco barn.

Indeed, the novel's principal theme and its plot resemble the Edenic model. The main subject is mortality, explored in the paired deaths of Mamie Talbot and Ginny Banning, in many supporting details, and in the epidemic, for which the townspeople hold Bull culpable. Likewise, the most dire consequence of Adam's sin was human mortality: "In the sweat of thy face shalt thou eat bread, till thou return unto the ground; for out of it wast thou taken: for dust thou art, and unto dust shalt thou return" (Gen. 3:19). The immediate punishment was expulsion: "Therefore the Lord God sent him forth from the garden of Eden. . ." (Gen. 3:23). Similarly, *The Last Adam's* plot culminates in a town meeting convened to oust George Bull from New Winton: " 'Throw him out!' " (p. 292). It is surely no accident that his replacement was to be a Doctor Moses (p. 280).

Readers, then, who expect allusions to Eden will find them, even though Cozzens borrows from Genesis mostly to disagree with it. In one way, however, the allusions are meant to reveal a substantial similarity between Bull and Adam. Adam and Eve, being the first humans, led a societyless existence; and Bull and Janet, indifferent to the town, approximate this asocial life. Janet's "indifference to talk in the village was so complete that George Bull doubted if she ever felt any of the pleasure he had in disregarding what was said. . . . In her . . . solitary existence, she was entirely free from the ceaseless obligations of maintaining whatever appearance you pretended to" (p. 35).

Without noting the Edenic implications, Frederick Bracher calls Bull "the antithesis of the 'social' man,"[11] and R. W. Lewis, quoting him, adds that an "interesting but frightening reading of Bull as the *last* Adam is the suggestion that our world breeds no more original creatures who are their own masters."[12] Here is one connotation that Cozzens probably meant his allusive title to have. Bull is Adamic partly in living as if there were no society.

Conflict in *The Last Adam* as social novel is between Bull—the nonconformist who enjoys a " 'simple life' " (p. 182), regards the town as " 'a bunch of bastards' " (p. 270), and has technical responsibility for the epidemic that makes everyone sick—versus New Winton, a society complete with boards, committees, political parties, churches, businesses, alliances, rivalries, snobberies, and so forth. The meeting to censure Bull epitomizes this conflict: " 'What are you going to do, George? Lick the whole town?' " (p. 291).

The answer turns out to be yes. Bull defies them all, bullies their meeting, outshouts them, and with Harris's ironic help, keeps his job. But George is a last solitary example. As he says, " 'They haven't had a real man in town since old Paul Banning died' " (p. 268). *The Last Adam* observes that the societyless condition of Eden was doomed. Glimpses into the telephone and power companies, the railroad, and Dr. Verney's medical practice show how modern life is organized. This condition may or may not be desirable, but it is surely inescapable. Organization can clean up "US6W's three-lane concrete . . . from Long Island Sound to the Massachusetts line" (p. 1). But organization is also the town meeting, the collective force of many weak, spiteful people into a spuriously democratic lynch mob that cannot resort to law, but can still ruin a man; except that, ironically, it can also be duped by a skilful demagogue like Harris into doing the opposite of what it intended, for blatantly fallacious reasons, and without knowing Harris's real motives at all. Cozzens does not choose between the individual who may have wronged the whole society by his mediocrity, and the mediocre society that nearly wronged him and—then deciding to keep him—got no more than it deserved.

But if an Adam is a man like George, ignoring society, then modern life has seen its last Adam. As the epidemic illustrates, no one is unaffected by his fellows. Mr. Banning thinks " 'It would be hard to show how his [Bull's] failings could possibly affect us' " (pp. 82–83), but Ginny's death by typhoid reveals his mistake. For better or worse, men in an intricately interdependent world will be social animals.

Mostly, however, Cozzens dwells on the dissimilarities between Bull and Adam. To that extent, the title as an Old Testament allusion is ironic, discrediting Biblical history, theology, and morality, and replacing them with deterministic counterparts. The irony, however, has often been overlooked. Many critics, most recently Pierre Michel, have referred, for instance, to George Bull's Adamic innocence: "The book ends with this image of an indestructible human being who is formidable in his Adamic innocence."[13] This is a perverse yet persistent misreading. George Bull is very far from innocent. Particularly in the Adamic sense, where innocence connotes the absence of carnal knowledge, the misreading is apparent, for George's carnality is town gossip. Adam was created "in the image of God" (Gen. 1:27), but Bull's enemies regard him as " 'an immoral godless' " man (p. 286), a " 'depraved old monster' " (p. 82); even Janet calls him " 'a confirmed old devil' " (p. 42) and an " 'old bastard' " (p. 314).

Bull had no Edenic innocence to fall from. He was seduced as Adam was, but he was not innocent beforehand: "His head was as active as most men's on the subject . . ." (p. 36). At the time, his innocence amounted to mere naïveté, he not realizing that "he could go anywhere, with or without proper reason . . ." (p. 39). His affair was soon known, yet he was never expelled from New Winton. Again, Cozzens contradicts the myth he alludes to.

That Bull neither has Adam's prelapsarian innocence, nor had it to lose, belongs within a more general scepticism about the myth as applied to any man. Cozzens broadens Bull's significance by observing that "Times had changed as much as he had, since [i.e., since 1903]; like himself, the age seemed to grow in experience. The naive sharp edge of shock and social outrage was gone from all the simpler improprieties" (p. 39). When Bull looks nostalgically back, the language suggests humanity longing for a paradise lost: "Remembering that holiday morning, it was possible to deduce from it and mourn a lost comfort, a lost ease and peace in the intimacy of small valley . . ." (p. 43). Completed, however, the passage does not imply man's loss of Eden and innocence; rather, it denies that mankind had either one to lose: "George Bull wasn't sure that such a land had ever actually existed, except on some summer or early fall days for an hour, or an afternoon. In the same fanciful way, life here seemed to him kind and friendly; the men were simple, but honest and happy. . . . Of course, the truth was that men were always the same everywhere" (p. 44).

Once Cozzens's scepticism is recognized, other Old Testament allusions make sense. The rattlesnake hunt, for example, alludes to Genesis, but surely does not *agree* with it. The serpent works Adam's ruin, but George Bull destroys the rattlesnakes which, in this realistic novel, are simply snakes—neither as harmless as rabbits (p. 158), nor as fatal as devils in disguise. (During the snake hunt Bull resembles several other legendary figures besides Adam: Aesculapius, the god of medicine, whose sacred symbol is the snake; Saint Paul and the viper of Melita (Acts 28:1–6); Saint George and the dragon, and by extension, Spenser's Red Cross Knight in *The Faerie Queene*.) The three men kill eight rattlesnakes, and although George is bitten by one, he kills it, too. His shout, " 'Here's one son of Satan who'll never see town!' " (p. 163), simultaneously alludes to Genesis and proclaims that the Biblical pattern has not held true. The joking allusion to Goldsmith's "Elegy on the Death of a Mad Dog" makes exactly the same point: " 'Snake bit me this morning,' he said, raising his right hand. 'The snake died' " (p. 167). Cozzens obviously enjoys setting the record straight. Genesis states that "the serpent was more subtil than any beast of the field" (Gen. 3:1), and after Bull kills the snake that bit him, Lester says, " 'I'll bet he wishes he hadn't been so smart' " (p. 164). Bull, a big healthy man, suffers neither more nor less than one would expect: " 'naturally it hurts, if that's what you mean. But I can eat all right' " (p. 165).

The expulsion, like the serpent, reveals discrepancies between myth and realistic novel. After Adam and Eve sinned, "they heard . . . God walking in the garden" and they "hid themselves" (Gen. 3:8). The Lord, noticing anyhow, expelled them, but Bull's experience revises this story. First, God does not put in an appearance. Second, God's place as the displeased overseer of the garden is now filled by the town's "superior" people (p. 39), the ironic deifying of whom occurs several times. Joe Tupping complains, " 'You keep saying, "Mrs. Banning herself," like she was God or something" (p. 52). In Mr. Banning's place, people would " 'think they owned the earth' " (p. 181). And Harris says sarcastically, " 'Suppose Doc Bull's not perfect? Who is? Well, . . . Herbert Banning's perfect, of course' " (p. 293). The irony of Mr. Banning as an ineffectual substitute for God in Eden is underscored both by his allegorical name and his constant puttering in his garden. Third, Bull does not hide from the social divinities: "Let them notice until they burst!" (p. 39). Instead, he carries on with Janet for years without being thrown out. The pattern repeats itself during the epidemic: Bull offends the social deity, which moves to expel him for his sins, but again it fails. In fact the expulsion motif is neatly reversed, Bull himself performing the book's two successful expulsions when he "tossed Joel out" of the school building (p. 230) and when he commits Mrs. Talbot to an asylum "To remove her cheaply and forever from human society" (p. 248).

Combining (a) Bull as the man strong enough to expel rather than be expelled, thus resisting the collective social force that easily masters a weaker person like Mrs. Jackson; and (b) Bull as the last man able to do so, we get an explanation for a social novel being named after an asocial man. For Bull commemorates independent men and also comments on the social types replacing them.

As an Edenic allusion, the title also questions the origin and nature of man. Again, Cozzens shows that men generally, and Bull in particular, are unlike Adam. Genesis asserts that Adam was created (a) by God, (b) in God's image, and (c) with dominion over the beasts. Mr. Cardmaker is Cozzens's most concise response: "When you saw him shaking and shifting the book held upside down, you saw, too, what James Cardmaker—his notes in the *Transcript,* his historic house and name, his college-educated daughter, aside—really was. Not merely evolved from, or like an ape, Mr. Cardmaker was an ape. The only important dissimilarities would be his relative hairlessness and inefficient teeth" (p. 37). This bluntly naturalistic definition of man—enriched by the irony that Mr. Cardmaker was an expert genealogist—contradicts the Biblical tenets that at first man was created (not evolved), that he bore the image of God (not of an ape), and that he had dominion over the beasts (rather than being one himself). By proliferating animal names (Herring, Vogel, Buck, Crowe, Bull), animal epithets (rat, goat, skunk, goose, hens, hog, babboons, elephant), and analogies between humans and beasts, Cozzens generalizes this passage about Mr. Cardmaker.

Man's animality is illustrated most fully in George Bull. Named after an animal, he feeds, drinks, moves, bathes, lusts, and roars like one. Janet says, " 'I could tell you a mile off. Harold thought it was an elephant upstairs' " (p. 32). When he and Janet head for a bedroom as cold as a barn, he says: " 'Wouldn't be the first barn we'd been in' " (p. 48). Called an old "horse doctor" (p. 56), he treats Janet's Devon cow, likening its mortality to his own (p. 87). But since he thrives (" 'The Bulls are long-lived' " [p. 88]) and the Devon dies, the better comparison is between George and Janet's prize bull: "Moloch III, moving with sullen majesty" was "the biggest Jersey bull she had ever seen; he must weigh more than fifteen hundred pounds. . . . Really, he was too good for this herd" (pp. 177–78). Immediately thereafter, Bull arrives and remarks that " 'Moloch looks pretty good out there' " (p. 178), making the juxtaposition unmistakable. It suggests that he has more in common with a bull named after a heathen god of sacrifice than with anyone created in the image of God.

Bull resembles a cave man as well as an animal. Thus he further undermines the myth that makes our ancestors Adam and Eve instead of simian primates. As Bull prepares for the rattlesnakes, Cozzens evokes Edenic images: the enmity with snakes suggests Genesis, and more subtly, so does "Love's Old Sweet Song,"[14] from which Bull is "Rumbling contentedly: *'Once in the dear dead days beyond recall—'* " (p. 156). The song's next line, which Cozzens omits, is "When on the world the mists began to fall. . . ." Echoing the "universal mist" passage (p. 127), it is another reference to Adam's creation: "there went up a mist from the earth . . ." (Gen. 2:6). Yet while Bull sings sentimentally about the dear dead days, he looks like a cave man: "He pawed through the closet" and produced "a roughly finished oak bludgeon," "a forked stick," and "a pair of worn leather gauntlets" (p. 156). In combination, Bull's primitiveness and animality add up, not to an Edenic life, but to " 'the simple life.' " Janet tells him, " 'You wouldn't have been bored anywhere on earth, so long as they had lots of food, and a little liquor, and a couple of women with their legs open,' " to which Bull assents, " 'Sure,' . . . 'the simple life!' " (p. 182).

Here is the opposite of the refinement to which the Bannings aspire. Mrs. Banning objects to Bull's "boorishness, his coarse, roaring manner, his callous, undoubtedly ignorant neglect of his work." Given her aristocratic notions of man and society, she might, by overlooking her own double meaning, find it "almost incredible that a family like the Bulls could have produced such a person!" (p. 69).

Indeed, many critics have also wondered why Cozzens, whose later books depict characters more refined than Bull, should have chosen such a man for a hero. Granville Hicks writes that Cozzens's "sympathy—surprisingly, it now seems—is with Doctor Bull."[15] According to Harry John Mooney, Jr., "That Cozzens himself to a large extent admires Dr. Bull seems certain."[16] Frederick Bracher calls Bull "the final admirable exemplar in Cozzens's novels of the fighting-cock hero."[17] R. W. Lewis, observing that Bull deviates "from practically every expectation of a hero," nevertheless concludes that "Bull is heroic."[18] R. P. Adams assures us that "it is plainly Dr. Bull . . . that Cozzens would have his readers admire."[19] These critics confuse what Cozzens depicts with what he admires. They mistake a protagonist for a hero.

Cozzens has commented, in a letter to me, on this question of heroes. To my remark that if he "meant for all of these later characters [protagonists in his novels since *The Son of Perdition* (1929)] to be seen more or less ironically, and not to be understood as heroes, then an awful lot of criticism has been dead wrong,"[20] Cozzens replied:

> Frankly I don't remember what Van Gelder or Du Bois[21]
> printed—but I'm sure I'd have said, late arrived-at but per-
> sisting, something to the effect that my writing idea had
> nothing to do with heroes or people admired or not
> admired—that is; I haven't anything to sell; just the egoistic
> hope that in setting down observations of life & people taught
> me by my own experience I can give readers Milton's "new
> acquist", useful or interesting to him. If you have Morning
> Noon & Night you'll find comment pp. 54–64; 401–404 that
> might help make what I mean clear. The result's that "an
> awful lot of criticism"—particularly the New (present)
> Establishment's—has been dead wrong because of attempts
> to find what isn't there; and not finding it, either denigrating
> the lack, or making out that it's really there only hidden
> through mean partisan bias or something.[22]

The applicability of this remark to *The Last Adam* is tidily established
by the phrase, "Milton's 'new acquist,' " referring to the passage
from *Samson Agonistes* that Cozzens quotes on p. 313 of the novel.

Knowing that Cozzens's "writing idea had nothing to do with
heroes or people admired or not admired" lets us understand Bull as
the author intended him. Whether Cozzens admires him is irrelevant to his purpose. He is, however, "setting down observations of
life & people." He observes what men essentially are, what they have
apparently evolved from, and what things really seem to influence
their survival. The naturalistic observation that these characters are
like animals illuminates their mortality better than Genesis does.

Innocence and obedience have nothing more to do with survival
in the epidemic than social station and wealth do. Guy Banning,
thinking of his sister, "whose purity or innocence he didn't exagger-
ate," nevertheless affirms that she "had it in the senses he considered
important" (p. 144). Larry Ward, by dint of his illicit relationship
with Charlotte Slade (p. 165), cannot claim such innocence. But
"The sickness, not respecting person or position" (p. 252), in pros-
trating forty people kills both Ginny with her innocence, and Larry
without his. In fact, Romans 2:11 and Ephesians 6:9 both assert that
there is no "respect of persons" with God. Cozzens has thus ascribed,
perhaps consciously, the attributes of an angry God to the typhoid.
Furthermore, in wealth and social standing, Ginny Banning and
Mamie Talbot are exact opposites. Yet they both die. The determi-

nant is neither moral, social, nor economic, but largely physical. As Bull explains about pneumonia, " 'Probably you either have the stamina to hang on while you develop resistance, or else you haven't. Mamie hadn't. Too puny' " (pp. 112–13). In their puniness, Ginny and Mamie are exactly alike. And on the other hand, "Girl like Geraldine would probably pull through fine. Got some meat on her' " (p. 113).

Bull, heftier than anyone else, survives the disease and the town's hostility. Refuting Genesis to the last, the novel closes by showing in Bull "Something unkillable. Something here when the first men walked erect; here now. The last man would twitch with it when the earth expired. A good greedy vitality . . ." (p. 314). Mentioning "first men," the passage evokes, not Adam, but our bestial ancestors, when they had first evolved to the stage of walking erect. In short, Cozzens alludes frequently to the Old Testament, but never confuses the myth of Eden with the facts of life. Neither does he moralize about what should survive. He simply gives us in George Bull a lusty example of what does.

Having considered Cozzens's complex use of the Edenic myth, readers who thought *The Last Adam* shallow may already be persuaded otherwise. Yet the title is only secondarily an Old Testament allusion, for it is quoted directly from I Corinthians 15:45:

> 44 It [the dead body] is sown a natural body; it is raised a spiritual body. There is a natural body, and there is a spiritual body.
> 45 And so it is written, The first man Adam was made a living soul; the last Adam was made a quickening spirit.
> 46 Howbeit that was not first which is spiritual, but that which is natural; and afterward that which is spiritual.
> 47 The first man is of the earth, earthy; the second man is the Lord from heaven.

The only critic to identify the source is R. W. Lewis,[23] who devotes a single sentence to it.

Even if Cozzens had not eventually confirmed the fact himself, there would be no doubt that I Corinthians 15:45 was his source. The phrase, "the last Adam," appears in only one verse of the New Testament,[24] and Cozzens quotes the very next one: "Doctor Wyck's voice reached her ears, proceeding urgently: 'Howbeit that was not first which is spiritual, but that which is natural; and afterwards that which is spiritual—' " (p. 149). Assisting readers who cannot locate this passage, the author virtually footnotes it: "Doctor Wyck had launched now on the long, resounding muddle following I Corinthians XV" (p. 147). The expression occurs in I Corinthians 15, the chapter named here; the Episcopal *Book of Common Prayer,* from which the minister is reading these scriptural passages, does include the expression; then comes the "muddle" (ironically very applicable to Ginny Banning) of Romans 8:14–39. Moreover, the novel's rejected title, "Bodies Terrestrial," can be found only five verses away (I Cor. 15:40): "There are also celestial bodies, and bodies terrestrial: but the glory of the celestial is one, and the glory of the terrestrial is another."

Indeed Cozzens is preoccupied with the fifteenth chapter of First Corinthians throughout the novel. May Tupping is shown reading from *Pilgrim's Progress,* where Bunyan, in describing Mr. Valiant-for-truth as he enters Heaven, quotes from I Corinthians 15 himself: " *'many accompanied him to the river side, into which as he went he said, Death, where is thy sting? And as he went down deeper, he said, Grave, where is thy victory? So he passed over, and all the trumpets sounded for him on the other side'* " (p. 5). Bunyan alludes to this famous text:

> 54 So when this corruptible shall have put on incorruption, and this mortal shall have put on immortality, then shall be brought to pass the saying that is written, Death is swallowed up in victory.
> 55 O death, where is thy sting? O grave, where is thy victory? (I Cor. 15:54–55)

Much later, as Mr. Banning comforts Bert Ward with banalities, he jeers at himself: "Then that solemn appeal to what Larry [Bert's dead brother] would understand! Did he mean to imply that Larry, in some better, happier world—Next he would be saying that the strife was o'er, the battle won!" (p. 272). Mr. Banning alludes to an Episcopal hymn called "Victory," which also derives from I Corinthians 15:

> The strife is o'er, the battle done,
> The victory of life is won;
> The song of triumph has begun.
> > Alleluia!
> Lord! by the stripes which wounded thee,
> From death's dread sting thy servants free,
> That we may live and sing to thee.
> > Alleluia! Amen.[25]

Allusions to I Corinthians 15 culminate in the final mention of Virginia Banning, it being another reference to the line, "O grave, where is thy victory?" Mr. Banning has sent a telegram, and Western Union reads it back: " 'Virginia died at half-past five today. Please come at once. Signed, Father. That name is, V as in victor, I as—' " (p. 313).

Clearly, then, Cozzens is conscious that the title's primary allusions to the New Testament are as ironic as those to the Old Testament. If he doubts the creation, fall from innocence, and expulsion, he is predictably sceptical also about virgin birth, redemption of sins, and especially triumph over death. Aware that such tenets cannot be empirically disproved, however, he resorts to frequent ironic insinuations of doubt.

Consider the gross physicality of the details surrounding Mamie Talbot's death. She is analogous, first, to Dr. Bull's other patient, the Devon cow, who also succumbs to pneumonia, "hopeless and helpless" (p. 33), on the same day. The "many cruelties of death" (p. 98) are evident in Mamie's "hideous, wasted" corpse (p. 99). Seeing her, May thinks of the undertaker's "grim fantastic art . . . which simulated peace or dignity in a corpse" (p. 99). Even Mamie's mother is horrified: "First, she would not sleep alone in a house with a dead body; then, she seemed to see it as more Mamie and less corpse. She would not leave Mamie all night alone" (p. 97).

Mamie's death generates much consciously irreligious writing. Bull, for instance, hears of it and realizes he'll have to go out, since " 'It's against the law to die around here without a certificate. All we need now's the enabling legislation and we'll live forever' " (p. 91). At the Talbots' house, Bull remains unabashed in the presence of death: " 'Get the body out as soon as you can, Howard. Not a very cheerful thing to have around' " (p. 113). He delights in puncturing hypocrisies, as when he tells his enemy, Emma Bates, to invite the offensive Mrs. Talbot home for lunch if she really wants to help; and when he openly relishes Mr. Banning's offer to settle Mamie's bill.

Ginny Banning has no more illusions about mortality or conventional Christianity than Bull has. Concerning her brother's " 'decency to be sorry,' " she says " 'What's it to Mamie? She's dead, isn't she?' " (pp. 95–96). During the sermon, Ginny can only scoff:

> To bury Mamie to such a strain really seemed absurd. . . . Who could imagine Mamie doing anything so resolute as, though she were dead, yet living? Where on earth would she get the nerve to see God for herself. . . ? Mamie, stretched

out, . . . would probably think that they were making fun of
her. As it is to the wise, a word to the weak is sufficient. Unless
you were proud, strong, well up in life, you had no need to be
reminded at such length that you were nothing and went
down like grass. Who could doubt it? (p. 147)

The funeral scene is ironic, for Ginny is close to her own death,
which, in fact, can be mistaken for the punishment of a God angry
about her blasphemies. Falling sick, she fears that her "touch of
influenza" may spoil her vacation. "Brooding on the possible malice
of fate so serving her, she had concluded that nothing could be more
like life or her luck." She adds that "probably there was a God.
Knowing that she regarded him as a lot of nonsense, God was always
on the alert to pay her sauciness with the inspired punishments of a
loving kindness" (pp. 188–89). Hence Ginny's prayer at the funeral
("*God, make it a week from Monday*" [p. 149]) and her glib contempt for
death (" 'Who wouldn't rather be dead than living in a hole like New
Winton?' " [p. 96]) seem sharply rebuked by the God who, a week
from Monday, apparently proves his existence by smiting her with
fatal (not merely inconvenient) typhoid. A theistical pattern appears
to have emerged.

Reconsidered, however, this reasoning falters. The moral pat-
ternlessness of fate is evident when Ginny's case is compared with
May Tupping's. At Mamie's funeral, Dr. Wyck reads, " 'Come, ye
blessed children of my Father, receive the kingdom prepared for
you from the beginning of the world—' " and "May looked sadly at
Albert with his spade, aware of the possible horrid irony in the
words, thinking how unlikely it was that anything remained for
Mamie except the earth Albert was waiting to shovel back" (p. 154).
May elsewhere has doubts just as penetrating as Ginny's. "Left to
herself, and to what she [May] could see of the universe, real and
ideal were lost together in an indifference so colossal, so utterly
indifferent, that there was no defining it. This immense mindless-
ness knew no reasons, had no schemes; there was no cause for it" (p.
210). And in general, "As long as she lived, she more or less expected
to realize that whatever was, was a pity" (p. 10). Thus, like Ginny,
May is another doubter who expects the worst, and for her faithless-
ness perhaps deserves it. Yet May's fate is utterly unforeseen and
happy. Cozzens thus implies that there is no discernible correspon-
dence between what one deserves and what one gets.

Confronted with religious explanations of fate, Cozzens probably shares May's sardonic attitude: she "reflected that the worst part of Mrs. Talbot's trouble was how little any of it was Mrs. Talbot's fault" (p. 207), but she adds that "you could see what a help it was to be able to believe all partial evil, universal good, or to feel sure that God was punishing Mrs. Talbot for offenses so cunning that He alone saw them. Your reason might revolt at it, but at least it would give the speculative mind some peace" (p. 208). When her reason revolts at religion, she is like George Bull. The son of a minister, George can now "see well enough what bad sense and worse logic the old man had once terrified him into considering wisdom" (p. 260).

One device to broaden this scepticism is the recurrent allusion to drowning. Just before he learns of Mamie's death, Bull is singing: " 'Crown Him with many crowns, The Lamb upon His throne; Hark! how the heavenly anthem drowns' " (p. 90). Interrupted here, the glorious line sounds grim, though actually, the hymn is another derivation from I Corinthians 15, celebrating the triumph over death:

> Hark! how the heavenly anthem drowns
>   All music but its own:
> Awake, my soul, and sing
>   Of him who died for thee. . . .
>
> Crown him the Lord of life,
>   Who triumphed o'er the grave,
> And rose victorious in the strife
>   For those he came to save;
> His glories now we sing
>   Who died, and rose on high,
> Who died, eternal life to bring,
>   And lives that death may die.[26]

Concerning Mamie's corpse, however, the image of drowning is again grim: "This way no one could miss the subtle record of her [Mamie's] last struggles, so terrible as they grew more surely vain, to get air; although unconscious in her stupor, to keep from drowning in her own clogged lungs" (p. 99). Elsewhere, Cozzens observes that "Drowning men do not complain of the great anguish caused by salt water flooding the bronchi" (p. 238). When Ginny dies, the image returns as her nurse despairs for "the great unfairness of this whole struggle. . . . You would think she [Ginny] lived on nothing but the breath painfully passed out through the cracked, parted lips. . . .

Now, now, must come, caught back, quick still, rough from the shades, the gasp in of air; life at once extended a little" (pp. 309–10). Given these persistently physiological, not spiritual, views of death, the Christian anthem does seem grimly drowned. Thus, when the telegraph operator reads back the message that Ginny has died— " 'That name is, V as in victor . . .' " (p. 313)—Cozzens seems to have answered Saint Paul's question by implying that the victory of the grave is, indeed, death.

When he is serious George Bull agrees, his awareness of mortality phrased in Pauline metaphors of conflict and triumph:

> Leadenly, he was aware of himself alive, and so, heavy hearted, of death—of when he would no longer be what he now wearily was. The evil destinies of man and the immense triumphs of death, seen so clearly at this bad hour, loaded him down. Discouragement, to feel death's certainty; exasperation, to know the fatuousness of resisting such an adversary—what was the use of temporary evasions or difficult little remedies when death simply came back and came back until it won?—moved him more than any personal dread of extinction. (pp. 87–88)

Discussion of the title's New Testament allusion leads back to Bull. Linked to the first Adam, he is connected just as certainly to "the last Adam," that is, Jesus. Saint Paul leaves no doubt about whether "the last Adam" is Jesus: "The first man is of the earth, earthy: the second man is the Lord from heaven" (I Cor. 15:47). As a Christ figure, Bull is splendidly ironic. Like Jesus, he is a healer. He jokes about being busy " 'Healing the sick' " (p. 179). Yet he performs no miracles: " 'The real trouble was, I forgot to put on a big show entitled "The Wonders of Science" ' " (p. 180). On the contrary, he often admits his medical helplessness, and some people maintain, " 'Just give him time, I say, and old Doc Bull can kill us all' " (p. 56). The resemblance between Bull and Jesus as healers is just strong enough to illuminate their enormous differences.

When Bull, wallowing in the tub, sings his hymns, the action is so diverting that readers can overlook the scene's title allusion. Bull, "in a mounting sense of his well-being," refers to "the last Adam" himself:

> Triumphant, at the top of his lungs, he handled the awkward English wording with agile malice. It made him think of bitter mornings, Michigan Christmases, maybe fifty years ago; but

he was never through being glad that they were over. "—Lo! He abhors not the Vir-r-gin's womb. Ver-er-y Gah-hod; be-gotten, not crea-a-ted. . . ." He snorted and wallowed again; he emerged, standing on his feet, caroling heartily. . . . He roared with pleasure; he knew plenty of hymns." (pp. 89–90)

The "Ver-er-y Gad-hod" in the second verse of *Adeste Fideles* is Jesus, being seen as the last Adam, who was "begotten"; not, like the first Adam, "created." Bull's "agile malice," though, suggests anything but a devout Christian's piety. The scene actually contrasts the message of salvation, which Bull sings but does not believe, to his own vitality, now abundantly reasserted, though the night before he was burdened with "Discouragement, to feel death's certainty" (p. 87).

The snake hunt tightens the bond between Jesus and George Bull. Symbolically dense, the scene culminates as Bull treats his own snake bite: "he drove the keen blade point in one line across the puncture; grunting, he crossed it remorsely with another line. Laying down the scalpel he fished out the chloride bottle . . ." (p. 163). In context, the religious possibilities of this crossed right thumb (not to mention the fishing out) are evident. But predictably, Cozzens turns the Christian symbols to ironic purpose, for ten pages later he writes: "to his own body he was old man Bull, hardly worth the effort. Cresting the swell of inflamed flesh, the angry crust of the still frail blood clot filled the criss-cross slash like a red mark of his certain mortality" (p. 174). In short, Cozzens confirms the symbolic connection between the cut and the Christian symbol, but mainly to deny the Christian meaning. Traditionally a promise of immortality, the cross has become instead a "mark of his certain mortality." Not the new man who will put on incorruption, George is "old man Bull," "old man" being a Scriptural synonym for Adam and his mortal descendants (as in Ephesians 4:22 and Romans 6:6). The cross identifies Bull, rather than anyone else, with the last Adam, but mainly to cast more doubts on the promised triumph over death.

Nevertheless, the book's closing paragraph simultaneously alludes to the title and involves Bull with the idea of immortality. A crucial passage frequently misread, it requires close attention. Janet observes Bull "grunting in the comfortable heat":

There was an immortality about him, she thought; her regard fixed and critical. Something unkillable. Something here when the first men walked erect; here now. The last man would twitch with it when the earth expired. A good greedy vitality, surely the very vitality of the world and the flesh, it survived all blunders and injuries, all attacks and misfortunes, never quite fed full. She shook her head a little, the smile half derisive in contemptuous affection. Her lips parted enough to say: "The old bastard!" (p. 314)

A troublesome problem is that the last paragraph has sometimes been misread to say that George himself is immortal. Pierre Michel thinks "The book ends with this image of an indestructible human being."[27] Frederick Bracher finds a "nostalgic portrayal of the vital, unkillable last Adam."[28] But read carefully, the passage asserts that the unkillable thing is the "good greedy vitality" that Bull has "about him." The man, of course, is not individually immortal. Bull himself speaks repeatedly of his own "certain mortality," and Cozzens would surely not deny it.

But in the most important sense, George Bull is meant to be a Christlike last Adam after all. Though the reference to "an immortality about him" seems to contradict the cross as a "mark of his certain mortality," it actually contains the paradox on which the whole book is built. For Bull, more than anyone else, embodies the "good greedy vitality, surely the very vitality of the world and the flesh," which "survived all blunders and injuries" (p. 314). Cozzens has shown us a naturalist's version of the salvation of man. It does not entail the transcendence of any individual's mortality. But passed on from first man to last, the vitality celebrated in George Bull makes mankind what it is, and largely determines the survival or extinction of the species.

6

R. H. W. DILLARD

Guard of Honor: Providential Luck in a Hard-Luck World

Guard of Honor was published in 1948, James Gould Cozzens's eleventh novel, his largest in size (631 pages) and scope (the workings of an entire Army Air Base and, by implication, of the entire United States Army in the second world war). It won the Pulitzer Prize for fiction that year and, after thirty years, remains in print in a Harvest edition. It has been treated intelligently and well by Cozzens's critics, especially by Frederick Bracher, Pierre Michel, and Harry John Mooney, Jr. in their books about Cozzens's work. But it has nevertheless not reached the level of serious attention and readership that it, at least to my mind, deserves. And I believe the reason for that lack of attention rests in the faulty classification of Cozzens as a "realist" and this novel as a document of social history.

Cozzens belongs to that generation of American writers that produced and developed "realistic" fiction to the fullest extent, a fiction of ostensibly objective observation, materialistic premises, and, as it turned out most often, enclosure and limitation and defeat. That fictive world is the world of Gatsby floating face down in his pool, of Julian English slumped down in the seat of his Cadillac, of Frederic Henry's "biological trap," of Temple Drake in the Luxembourg Gardens in "the season of rain and death," of Captain Clendening in "a sort of mental stupor" supporting himself on the rail of the bridge of the sinking S.S. *San Pedro.* It is a world we all have seen and shared when our eyes are cold and clear, one that tempts us constantly to accept it as "reality," the product of an illusionless rendering of the hard, bare facts of life.

We have come to see finally that the best writers of that generation, the Faulkners and Hemingways, and those we discovered a bit late like Nabokov and Borges, were not victims of that reductionist definition and those hard facts at all, that they produced a literature of freedom and value in the very context of enclosure, limitation, and defeat. They all found something to hold to and build upon that denied the traps of materialism and its entropic understanding. *Guard of Honor* and the work of Cozzens in general attain that larger vision but with such subtlety and honesty and adherence to the surface details of ordinary experience that it has simply not been noticed by many of his readers or by any of those critics who have chosen to label him as the most conservative spokesman of his generation, using as a basis for this judgement those same ways of narrow seeing and saying that he transcends in his work.

In a letter to the English publisher of *Guard of Honor*, Cozzens admits that he "would just have to write off as readers everyone who could not or would not meet heavy demands on his attention and intelligence, or lacked the imagination to grasp a large pattern and the wit to see the relation which I could not stop to spell out between this & that."[1] Any reader who will not respond to Cozzens's "heavy demands" would, as doubtless many did and do, see the novel in much the same way that Judge Schlichter, a character in the novel, sees life itself—as "mostly a hard-luck story, very complicated, beginning nowhere and never ending, unclear in theme, and confusing in action."[2] *Guard of Honor* is just that hard-luck story, the account of life, as Colonel Ross in the novel describes it, in a world "of complicated effects from simple causes, of one thing stubbornly leading to another" (p. 51). It is all that, but it is much, much more.

Judge Schlichter, who is, appropriately enough, dead when the novel takes place and is only remembered by Colonel Ross, the conscience of the novel and of the characters in it, shared the hypocritical values of the last generation of the nineteenth century—a hollow vision of human failure masked by moral platitudes and pious stances. The judge was fond of quoting Pope on universal harmony whenever the failings and limits of human living thrust themselves into his attention. But behind those platitudes lurked the real horror, the vision of a mechanical world without purpose or point, the classic hard-luck story of living in the material world:

> Unhappy victims complained of their unhappy circumstances. The trusting followers of the misjudged easiest way

found that way immediately getting hard. Simple-minded aspirants, not having what it took, did not quite make it. Conceited men proudly called their shots and proceeded to miss them, without even the comfort of realizing that few attended long enough to notice, and fewer cared. Any general argument or intention was comically contravened in reported or portrayed dispensations by which the young died and the old married; courageous patience overdid it and missed the boat; good Samaritans, stopping, found it was a trap and lost *their* shirts, too—everyday incidents in the manifold pouring-past of the Gadarene swine, possessed at someone's whim, but demonstrably innocent—for what was a guilty pig, or a wicked one?—to the appointed steep place. Though so sad, the hard luck often moving, it was a repetitious story, and long; and what did it prove? Let somebody else figure that out! (pp. 534–35)

Schlichter's world is one of insulted and injured innocence that clings to lost ideals and at the same time reduces the living world to a repetitious and empty joke, a tired jest "at someone's whim" and at everyone's expense.

At first glance, the world of the novel, of Ocanara Army Air Base in Florida in 1943, seems to be precisely that world described by Judge Schlichter, a complex pattern of lost chances and hard luck. The novel moves from a near accident to a genuine and fatal catastrophe through a series of apparently random events, all influencing each other, all stubbornly leading from one to another. The flow of events moves up and down the hierarchical structure of the army command, ensnaring generals and lieutenants, men and women, heroes and fools. Good men behave badly, and bad men stand up for good causes. And all the while the "teapot tempest" at Ocanara swirls and puffs, the larger reality of the war continues, rendering those chaotic events at once more absurd and more genuinely and poignantly real. As the ridiculous and deeply serious battle over the right of black officers to use the Area Officers Club rages, "now, at this very moment, if the weather had been at all possible, Eighth Air Force bombers were turning, a certain number of them damaged with engines out and dead and wounded on board, to try to make their English bases. Perhaps also at this very moment . . . Fifth Air Force fighters were dropping belly tanks as the Zeros came climbing at them over some formerly unimportant Indonesian harbor" (p. 318).

The war is real, and Ocanara seems unreal, some midsummer

night's dream; three of the lakes around the air base are, for that matter, named Titania, Oberon, and Thisbe. But Ocanara is, for all its absurdity, quite as real as the war, complete with war casualties— paratroopers dropped to their deaths during a celebration of General Beal's birthday, drowned in Lake Lalage. General Nichols had jokingly suggested the proper course for a paratrooper, upon discovering that conditions made a landing look bad: "Why, unless the man's a bloody fool, he climbs back into the plane and tries somewhere else" (p. 399). But, of course, in the real chaos of Ocanara and our world, the joke fails and all men are bloody fools—Schlichter's truth. As Colonel Ross puts it, "you will not do what you cannot do. . . . Gravity is a condition, not a theory" (p. 439). And quite fitting to the absurdity of the world of which he speaks, he is talking, before the catastrophe, only metaphorically about the problem of the black officers and the Officers Club. Schlichter's world, indeed.

The easiest response to such a world, easier even than Schlichter's own platitudes and quotations, is to surrender, to give in to randomness and emptiness and despair. Captain Nathaniel Hicks, before his one-night adulterous encounter with Lieutenant Amanda Turck, finds himself on the edge of making that easy and deadly response:

> It was just the still-incredulous amazement that this should be here and that this should be he. Pinching himself would do no good. It was not necessary; he felt already his cold, unconfused wide-awakeness, hopeless and helpless in its sense of time's great length; of all yesterdays gone; of life like this, and this war, lasting on and on; of the intolerable permanence of a situation which had been his, it seemed, not eighteen months but all of eighteen years, and from which he would be delivered, at this rate, never. (p. 590)

Others in the novel face that same temptation, that sly invitation to accept Schlichter's world at face value and to surrender to it. General Bus Beal, the hero of the novel, faced that temptation in 1941 and early 1942 in the Philippines, "the nightmare of everything going down in ruin around you (men wept at Nichols Field when the parked B–17's blew to bits or sank to junk in the flames of oxidized aluminum and running gasoline); your friends killed; your country shamed; disaster heaped on disaster; death at every turn; nothing to fight with; nothing to hope!" (p. 19). He had conquered it then, but he must face it again at Ocanara, wrapped more insidiously in the backwater absurdities of a training field instead of a fighting front. The continual recurrence of the opportunity for despair is at the tragic center of Schlichter's realistic world. Colonel Woodman at Sellers Field, facing the same pressures as Beal, commits suicide; Beal's own surrender is less explosive, but just as real: "Something had gone out of him; some distinguishing inner mettle, a sustained tension of nerves, a spirit wound up to act; something so much a part of Bus that it was hardly noticeable, taken for granted" (p. 315). Like Achilles, General Beal sulks in his tent, not in anger or injured pride but in guilt and self-doubt, trapped in Schlichter's world as inexorably as Captain Hicks in his morning's anguish or Colonel Woodman in his fatal despair.

If all of this were the sum of *Guard of Honor,* it would be only a rather long and cynical addition to the ranks of the ordinary realistic novel, a heavyweight *Mister Roberts* or military *The Old Wives' Tale,* a detailed account of that endless "pouring past . . . to the appointed steep place." But, as I said before, it is much, much more.

In the letter to his English publisher, Cozzens said that "What I wanted to write about here, the essence of the thing to be said, the point of it all, what I felt to be the important meaning of this particular human experience, was its immensity and its immense complexity."[3] Not its overwhelming complexity, but its *immense* complexity; not its absurdity, but its *immensity.* In Schlichter's hard-luck world, no one is able to see life whole: "Some of it you saw yourself, and while that was at most very little, you could piece out the picture, since it always fitted in with what other people said they saw" (p. 534). But Cozzens's world is more immense than that, for with its immensity comes a larger sense of life and purpose beyond the immediate confusions facing each individual in it. "I wanted to show," he continued in the letter to the English publisher, "the peculiar effects of the inter-action of innumerable individuals functioning in ways at once determined by and determining the functioning of innumerable others—all in the common and in every case nearly helpless involvement in what had ceased to be just an 'organization' . . . and became if not an organism with life and purposes of its own, at least an entity, like a crowd."

In Cozzens's world, the individual is at once small and nearly helpless, unable to see or to act freely, and at the same time an organic (or at least possibly so) member of a larger movement in life which is purposive and does have direction. This is not Schlichter's or the mechanistic realist's confused and hopeless world, but is rather one akin to that once described by Emerson in his essay, "Experience":

> The results of life are uncalculated and uncalculable. The years teach much which the days never know. The persons who compose our company converse, and come and go, and design and execute many things, and somewhat comes of it all, but an unlooked-for result. The individual is always mistaken. He designed many things, and drew in other persons as coadjutors, quarrelled with some or all, blundered much, and something is done; all are a little advanced, but the individual is always mistaken. It turns out somewhat new and very unlike what he promised himself.[4]

This (to use Arthur Koestler's word) holonic nature of man is the key to Cozzens's world and to our own. We are at once small and helpless and isolate and at the same time organically of the whole, large and developing and valuable. Colonel Ross, during his long meditation which is the intellectual center of *Guard of Honor* states the problem and the answer in terms that Emerson would surely approve.

The problem:

> There never could be a man so brave that he would not sometime, or in the end, turn part or all coward; or so wise that he was not, from beginning to end, part ass if you knew where to look; or so good that nothing at all about him was despicable. This would have to be accepted. This was one of the limits of human endeavor, one of those boundaries of the possible whose precise determining was . . . the problem. (p. 532)

The answer:

> Downheartedness was no man's part. A man must stand up and do the best he can with what there is. If the thing he labored to uncover now seemed in danger of stultifying him, could a rational being find nothing to do? If mind failed you, seeing no pattern; and heart failed you, seeing no point, the stout, stubborn will must be up and doing. A pattern should be found; a point should be imposed. Was that too much? . . . Once you knew you needed something to keep you operative, playing the man, you could be of good heart. Your need

would find it for you, and adapt it to you; and even support
you in it, when those who had different needs, or thought
they had none, asked if you were crazy. (p. 534)

Colonel Ross knows that this is no new answer, but he also knows
that it is the only honest answer—knows it intuitively and rationally.
Henry Worthington, the narrator of *Morning Noon and Night,* refers
to Christ's comment on the same problem, much more succinctly
put, but saying in even larger terms the same thing: "Why callest
thou me good? None is good, save one, that is, God." There is the
truth, a truth that Colonel Ross can see and act upon. "Old Schlichter," however, "weighed what he got from hypocrisy against what he
might hope from honesty. He let honesty go. He did not have the
nerve to be honest" (p. 531). Cozzens does have the nerve.

Guard of Honor is an open and honest examination of a complex of
human failings, but unlike so many of its realistic counterparts, it is
also a celebration of human strength and of those larger values that
give hope and meaning to the living world. It is an *Iliad,* a modern
one that finds precisely the same heroic strength in a morally eddy-
ing backwater of the war that Homer found in the actual fighting in
his war. It is built upon General Beal's loss of mettle and his recovery
of it, a recovery triggered by a pattern of events so interrelated and
complex that it requires the whole of this large novel to relate it.

Beal, the war hero who behaved heroically in the face of astonish-
ing odds in the Philippines and in New Guinea in the early months of
the war, bears a burden of guilt with him to his new post in Florida so
far from the action his nature seems to require. He chose himself as
the one flier most likely to be able to get a message out from Bataan
to Mindanao, to "leave his surviving friends to the Japanese . . . [to]
escape, if he could, to life and health, to food and comfort; to honors
and promotions" (p. 21). He made the right decision, but the guilt,
whether he is consciously aware of it or not, remains. "It was fair to
believe that General Beal knew no more about himself than most
men; and, out of his self-knowledge, could tell you, no matter how
hard and honestly he tried, less than you could learn from what you
saw or heard of his behavior" (p. 20). He does not analyze himself,
but he does respond to things within as well as without, to worries
and doubts about the past as well as thoughts and actions in the
present.

The event that triggers his crisis of lost mettle occurs on the
Thursday that opens the novel, but already the problem has been

gnawing away within him. He has not slept with his wife for two
weeks before that day. He does not know why any more than we do,
but clearly his guilt and his frustration at being in a bothersome and
not very rewarding backwater of the war are involved. When, while
flying an AT–7 he had commandeered from a very upset Colonel
Woodman at Sellers Field, he nearly collides with a B–26 at Ocanara
and freezes at the controls, allowing his copilot, Lieutenant Colonel
Benny Carricker, to save the day, his crisis becomes conscious and
immobilizing. The complications mount as Carricker assaults and
seriously injures the black pilot of the B–26, as the other black pilots
on the base stage a protest about their being kept illegally out of the
Officers Club, as Colonel Woodman in his anger and despair commits suicide, as General Nichols arrives from Washington to give a
Distinguished Flying Cross to the very pilot that Carricker had
attacked, and as Beal's birthday celebration turns into the catastrophe with the paratroop jump.

It is easy enough to see, even from that extremely simplified and
inadequate summation, something of the nature of Beal's crisis. It is
serious and potentially damaging to the base as a whole and ultimately to the war effort and thereby to the entire world. And that
crisis is resolved; it is resolved in part by Beal himself, who finds the
"something to keep you operative" of Ross's answer, and in part by
Ross, who acts for Beal when he cannot act for himself, and in part by
the force and pattern of the whole ungraspable complex of events
occurring in Ocanara and around the world during the three days it
takes to bring that resolution about. Beal goes aloft with Carricker
and mock-dogfights himself back into action; Ross resolves the question of the black officers with restraint and with the best wisdom he
can muster at the moment; the tragedy of the paratroop jump brings
Beal to tears and frees him from old guilts, thus enabling him to face
future responsibilities. And all of those forces are brought together
by something.

Behind all that elaborate pattern of motivation and causation
there is something else at work, an acausal connecting principle that
weaves these men and events together, men who are not good,
events that are not clear, to produce a resolution that at least seems to
be to the advancement, moral and practical, of all concerned. Colonel Ross first notices it when, much to his own surprise, he finds
himself pronouncing these lines from *Samson Agonistes:* "*All is best
though we oft doubt what the unsearchable dispose of Highest
Wisdom brings about, and ever best found in the close. Oft He seems*

to hide His face, but unexpectedly returns, and to His faithful champion" (p. 524). Carl Jung and Wolfgang Pauli would possibly call it synchronicity; Henry Worthington would call it providence; Colonel Ross calls it luck.

Early in the novel, Ross thinks about General Beal as a lucky man. "There are, or seem to be, forces affecting a man's life wholly outside a man's control," and he believes that Beal "might feel that he owed his chances to use them to something outside, rather than something inside, himself" (p. 16). He goes on to speculate on the close relationship between greatness and luck:

> Because he found himself meeting . . . emergencies adequately or more than adequately, General Beal might be right in holding himself, humbly, no more than a lucky fellow. Colonel Ross, too, thought (that being how it was) that General Beal was lucky. Anyone was lucky who could go a successful way without the call to exercise greatness, without developing greatness's enabling provisions—the great man's inner contradictions; his mean, inspired inconsistencies; his giddy acting on hunches; and his helpless, not mere modest acceptance of, but passionate, necessary trust in, luck. (p. 17)

By the end of the novel, Beal has become more than just a lucky fellow; he has begun to trust in his luck and to approach, quite possibly, greatness. He expresses his new confidence in his suggested agreement with Colonel Ross that (in answer to Schlichter's repeated question, *"sed quis custodiets ipsos custodes?"*) Beal and Ross "pick up after" each other.

> I have some little weaknesses, like having to do things my way; and Jo-Jo [General Nichols] thinks I'm just a fly-boy, and I am. No, I'm not any master mind; but spell it out for me and I'll pretty often get it. You tell me what you think I don't know, and I'll tell you what I think you don't know; and we'll get there. . . . I'll do the best I can, Judge; and you do the best you can; and who's going to do it better? (p. 631)

Ross and Beal have, together, reached a turning place, not just for themselves, but for all those around them and, given their direct involvement in the world war, with the whole world. The individual at this moment is no isolated, small, trapped victim in a world of reductionist defeat; he is rather the hero in a living world, one like that described by William James:

Our acts, our-turning places, where we seem to ourselves to
make ourselves and grow, are the parts of the world to which
we are closest, the parts of which our knowledge is the most
intimate and complete. Why should we not take them at their
face-value? Why may they not be the actual turning-places
and growing-places which they seem to be, of the world—why
not the workshop of being, where we catch fact in the making,
so that nowhere may the world grow in any other kind of way
than this?[5]

Guard of Honor, as John P. Marquand suggested upon its publication, is a "fine, almost a definitive picture of life as it was led by the
American Army Air Force in World War II,"[6] but it is also a fine
picture of the life of the world, of the process of its growth. It is a
world in which gravity is a condition, in which limitations impose
themselves upon human freedom continually, but it is also one in
which downheartedness is not necessarily a resultant condition, in
which growth and change and providential luck are at the heart of
human values and human experience.

The novel opens in General Beal's AT–7 in which, although "time
was passing," the plane "seemed stationary . . . hung at perpetual
dead center in an immense shallow bowl of summer haze" (p. 3). The
plane descends into the world with the startling shock of the near
accident, and the novel descends with it into a seeming chaos of
motion and hard luck. General Beal's mock dogfight with Carricker
draws that descent back up into the air, this time with purposive (if
playful) action, far from stationary; it prepares him for the terrible
descent of the doomed paratroopers and his own rebirth into action
on the earth as well as in the air. At the novel's end, General Beal and
Colonel Ross stand together in the night, looking after General
Nichols's departing plane: "The position lights of the northbound
plane could still be made out by their steady movement if you knew
where to look. The sound of engines faded on the higher air,
merging peacefully in silence. Now in the calm night and the vast
sky, the lights lost themselves, no more than stars among the innumerable stars" (p. 631). That beautiful passage is the appropriate end
for this rich novel, a peace well earned, the higher air, a belonging of
man and his actions in the vital context of the innumerable stars.

Our sense of our place in the world around us has changed and is
changing so very radically that most of the major works of ordinary
realistic fiction seem almost irrelevant today. During the time I have

been writing this essay, the Viking landers have been scooping up Martian soil and sending us photographs of a new world we have never seen before except in dreams, physicists have discovered yet another particle in the nucleus of the atom which leads them to believe that the number of such particles may be infinite, Har Gobind Khorana succeeded in fashioning a man-made gene that functions normally in a living cell, Raymond Moody's and Elizabeth Kübler-Ross's research findings on the experience of life after death are appearing in almost every journal, and Johan Bjorksten and Rolf Martin have announced their belief that they will discover an enzyme soon that will add eighty years to individual human life expectancy. Each day some basic premise of our understanding of ourselves and our relationship to the rest of being is completely transformed. A fiction rigidly rooted in the old premises of reductionist thought fades rapidly from day to day.

I have certainly not exhausted the richness of *Guard of Honor* or of Cozzens's approach to fiction or of his sense of providential luck in this brief essay, but I do hope that I have indicated with some suasion that he is no fading ordinary realist, but rather an honest and lasting artist, whose work thrives and will continue to thrive on the force and power of his intelligence and imagination—call it wisdom, or, call it his "passionate, necessary trust in, luck."

7

R. V. CASSILL

The Particularity of
Guard of Honor

As years separate us farther from World War II and addle or correct memory with reconsiderations as well as forgetfulness, this novel— at any rereading—increasingly startles the eye with the shock of anomaly. To read it now is like coming on finely composed and detailed photos of Pompeiian life among vestigial and flaking wall paintings and the theoretical reconstructions of archaeology. Whatever else is to be said of it, the novel's exactitude of representation is the point from which we perforce begin.

The extreme resolution of detail (to continue the optical, photographic simile) distinguishes Cozzens's achievement from the loose, familiar category of the realistic war novel. The once over-touted realism of *The Red Badge of Courage* seems the tough-minded fantasy of an inexperienced youth by comparison, and whatever their naturalistic merits or invocations of pity, terror and fatal grandeur, neither *War and Peace, A Farewell to Arms* nor *The Naked and the Dead* tell us what our sight and hearing would have discerned in a military surrounding as *Guard of Honor* does.

When court martial is contemplated the Charge Sheets are identified as WDAGO Form No. 115—printed to Colonel Ross's annoyance (he recognizing that in the ordinary course of things they will be often handled) on poor quality paper. When three WAC officers sit down to breakfast in an officers mess located where the logic of base engineers and post commanders would in fact place it, Cozzens tells us what each ate, accommodating their fictional consumption of food to their physical size, fundamental character, state of psychic absorption or distraction, *and* the menu that would indeed have been available for breakfast in an officers mess in the State of Florida. The big WAC captain, eating more slowly than her two lieutenants and eating more, is deeply absorbed in the latest instructions governing insignia to be worn on the WAC uniform, and those instructions are, in spirit and detail, exactly rendered while she drops muffin crumbs on her "immaculate khaki shirt." When the range officer speaks by radio to the unidentified pilot firing at the gunnery targets from a P–47, he admonishes the flier to remember that his guns are "bore-sighted for two seven zero miles per hour." Do I know that at this particular period of the war the guns of the model of the P–47 then in service were, in fact, so adjusted to the speed of the plane? I do not. But I know the considerations involved in plane design and handling are those that would pertain and would fall within the purview of the range officer. And being so assured by the accuracy of hundreds of other specifications within the novel, I have no choice but to believe those that lie beyond the present possibility of verification. The picture is reliable to a degree surpassing historical report, vivid in a fashion that cannot fade as more subjective renditions are prone to do.

Yet all this detailed, coherent and inherently credible specification might be underrated as merely mechanical accuracy if the details, the ultimate particles of Cozzens's art, were not so shrewdly sorted and combined into the large scene he creates and the variegated characters he peoples it with. Page by page we can discern the manner of his approach; it is not quite so easy to define the intention of the work as a whole, though we may be fairly sure that in his comprehensive aims, as in the particulars, representational objectives have a priority over thematic ones.

Did he, then, project so large a design in order to represent schematically the whole of what he calls the "heteromorphic and fantastical Army of the United States?" I think not. Vast as his design may be, we are in no way encouraged to think it is anything but a part of processes and historic dispositions much vaster yet.

Within the Thursday, Friday, and Saturday which comprise the whole chronology of his novel (excepting rare flashbacks and certain historical information delivered in dialogue), we are shown precisely delimited fragments of the lives of many ranks, male and female, with their dependents and some transient civilians, who do their country's business on Ocanara Air Base. But the author's almost ferocious commitment to particularity still restrains the reader from assuming that even this extraordinary sum of participating characters looks quite like a "cross-section" of the American military. The days of the action fall within a particular period of the war effort; allusions to global strategy, the state of the military art and weapons technology are as carefully adjusted to the *moment* of history, as what they ate for breakfast is tuned to the personalities of Captain Burton and Lieutenants Lippa and Turck. Attitudes and practices relative to the employment of black personnel—and much of the action of the novel takes its shape from these—are in a state of transition. Something is lost if we try to read the "race problem" of black Lieutenant Willis as typical of the evolving prejudices of the era. As much is lost if we take General Beal (commanding at Ocanara) to be a synthetic and idealized composite of "the Commanding General"— as, say, General Cummings is in Mailer's *The Naked and the Dead.* Or if we take Beal's wife Sal as a typical army brat and army wife.

The panoramic, hour-by-hour development of the drama unfolding among the multitude of implicated characters on the air base is simply too large, shaggy, distorted by impulse, contingency, and individual quantitative dynamics to be fitted under the cliché umbrella (dear to hasty readers who want "the gist" and only the gist) of *microcosm.*

Neither microcosm of the global war effort nor cross-section of the United States Army, this novel represents vastness as we actually experience it—in the power of a crowded scene charged with conflict—and refuses the reductions of conceptual thought which always imply the superiority of the universal to the particular.

Once and somewhere—*only* once and at the Ocanara Air Force Base called AFORAD, Air Force Operations and Requirements Analysis Division—the wife of a Major General Commanding may have said, when her playful husband twisted her wrist, " 'No! Fins! I quit. Jo-Jo, make him stop! *Ira!* Everybody's looking at us! I'll kick your shins—.' " And only once and somewhere, in the heat of a Florida afternoon, may a WAC lieutenant have quoted Milton, " 'The Lybian air adust.—' " (when "Lybian" must have, on one of its highly charged levels of contemporary ambiguity, invoked the tank battles in the Libyan desert), but in the scheme of values and realities proposed and sustained by Cozzens's art, this stark uniqueness of the event, the word and the person shows as something more poignant than the epiphanies and concrete universals that make the experience of the race seem so disposable. Without direct allusion

Cozzens reminds us of Whitman's declaration: "The American compact is altogether with individuals." Which means, if we can still puzzle it out, that the discrete soul and body, the discrete and unrepeatable event, are first in our concern. The point of Cozzens's technique, and his unflagging adherence to its limits, thus would seem to be a reaffirmation of a principle central in Whitman's vision.

There are, to be sure, ruminative and philosophically searching passages in this novel built of appearances and unique events. Most of the reflective passages are the speculations of Col. Norman Ross, who is the closest thing to a Central Intelligence we get. Among Ross's exemplars and objects of scrutiny there is the figure of the visiting General Nichols, emissary of Hap Arnold, CG of the Air Force, and thus the spokesman for the "larger concerns" that play on and from Ocanara Air Base. In Ross's approving judgment, Nichols is a man who looks out "calmly, in well-earned assurance of rightly estimating the possibilities and limitations of the Here and Now, and so of being ready for what might come."

Dedication to and adequacy for the unique present is thus articulated (as it is implied by the technique and its accomplishments) as the zenith of the human potential. As in other Cozzens novels, notably in *By Love Possessed,* adequacy to the moment is the greatest of realistic ambitions. As Thomas Mann put it once, "History is ordinary reality, into which we are born and to which we must be adequate." A very traditional view, admitted by Col. Ross not to be "wholly satisfactory"—the idea that "wisdom, though better than rubies, came to so little; that a few of the most-heard platitudes contained all there was of it; that its office was to acquaint you not with the abstruse or esoteric, but with the obvious, what any fool can see. . . ."

Such primary dedication to the transient and the obvious may be, for all we know and for all Cozzens knows, the default to despair that romantics and reformers declare it to be. An individual character, Col. Ross, may refuse to consider it such. "Downheartedness was no man's part. . . . If mind failed you, seeing no pattern; and heart failed you, seeing no point, the stout, stubborn will must be up and doing. A pattern should be found; a point should be imposed. Was that to much?"

The very structure of the novel—if not its final and quietly nihilistic sentence—reminds us that the "will" here invoked is purely personal and as transient as everything else, though with Col. Ross it may be an habitual stay. As for its effect beyond the here and now, nothing is to be said for it. It is Ross's destiny merely to *watch* the "persistent children" who have their fingers on the levers of military and media power, not

> even despising them. . . . They had the means and resources of man's estate. They were more dextrous and much more dangerous than when they pretended they were robbers or Indians; and now their make-believe was really serious to them. You found it funny or called it silly at your peril. Credulity had been renamed faith. Each childish adult determinedly bet his life and staked his sacred pride on, say, the Marxist's ludicrous substance of things only hoped for, or the Christian casuist's wishful evidence of things not so much as seen. Faiths like these were facts. They must be taken into account; you must do the best you could with them, or in spite of them.

The "best" that can be done, however, is merely and simply what *was* done and what *is* done. The philosophic overview provided by Col. Ross comes to just the same thing that the novel in its bulk and bustle, color and light, declares: Life is a tale told by the wise and the idiotic, signifying nothing.

But, of course, the tale tells us there is purpose, anxiety, gratification, courage, deception in all those individual lives that run from any given Thursday to any given Saturday and that, though it is impossible to "seize the day" or even the moment, still the multitude of temporary warriors at Ocanara reach out hands and hearts in a miracle of fidelity to their individual roles. No meaning but that miracle, says the novel.

A dispersal of value and significance into the individual and the transient—this is not only what Cozzens is writing about but also celebrating. And such celebration is one of the noblest justifications of the novel altogether. It is our great antidote against the reductive idealism that wants to close the human account as soon as its fundamental principle is perceived. The true novelist wants his novel to be adequate to the reportage of the "broadcast doings of day and night." Let themes and theses—even those shaped so judiciously by Col. Ross—be whirled along in the flux where "the lights lost themselves, no more than stars among the innumerable stars."

Yet for all its dynamic insistence on the atoms and the flux, its denial, in effect, of intelligible patterns, *Guard of Honor* is a tightly patterned book. There is a major paradox in this. Again we will find,

I think, that it is just *the* paradox that the novelistic imagination is designed to express.

There is, in an obvious way, a tight pattern of action. When Benny Carricker most irresponsibly strikes a black junior officer—who is, in fact, scheduled to be decorated at Ocanara by generals visiting from Washington—a chain of events is set in motion that will involve, in direct or indirect fashion, nearly all the individual characters who appear in the novel. Though the plot actions are dispersed in small fractions and the roles played in the resolution of the plot are extraordinarily distributed among the personnel of the base, the overall plot is both sturdy and lucid.

It is the function of the plot to bind extravagant diversity into unity—and to link in meaningful paradox the propositions that while the men and women on the air base are most intelligible in their individuality, *still* what they *do* is most intelligible when they are fused into a collectivity with a singular objective.

The will that fuses them is nothing very mystical. Certainly, in concept, it is not the will of the peoples that Tolstoy tried so manfully and gropingly to define in *War and Peace*. It is, simply put, the will of the United States to make war effectively on its antagonists. *Guard of Honor* demonstrates the elaborate pattern by which that will flows through one of the institutions created to implement it—how it is broken down, relayed, diverted, transformed, and finally recomposed and directed onward once more.

Power flows through channels and tributaries of communication, and it is the triumph of Cozzens's virtuosity to show that the individuals who distort the signals they receive are at the same time the instruments for restoring the essential significance of the transmitter. The apparent chaos, the confusion of tongues, is shown to make, after all, an unambiguous unit of sense. The institution, after all, accommodates the variable qualities and impulses of its components.

Warrant Officer Botwinick conceives himself to be the nerve center through which will pass all the essential information necessary to implement the functioning of the base. Symbolically and literally ambidextrous, he receives, correlates and disperses a great mass of intelligence, ranging from information supplied by company spies to directives from Washington. Yet Cozzens shows that Botwinick's own estimate of his function is illusory. The nerve center is no more, if no less, necessary to the whole web of communication that directs power than is peripheral gossip. How Botwinick deliberately falsifies a part of the information that has flowed to him—and how his superiors tolerate or cover up his misfeasance—makes an amusing turn of the action. But such willful obstruction of information and justice is in no way decisive by itself. How the story of Carricker's assault is revamped and fed back into the power stream by the liberal prejudices of Lt. Edsell is similarly not decisive. The interventions and dirty tricks of the local press, the imminent intervention by the national press, the interpretation and orders given by officers in positions of authority, the tonal shifts provided by those responsible for public relations, the peripheral modifications fed in by those indirectly concerned—like General Beal's wife—none of this is decisive either. What Cozzens finds is that at some level there is a system of checks and balances that comes into operation without being invoked—which comes into play, in fact, without being recognized by any of those who wish for it or dread it.

Using the instrument of the novel, adjusting it so it makes visible the real checks and balances in the institutions that transmit collective power—to show the uniqueness of each individual and at the same time his instrumentality within the collective, there is the real excellence of this fiction, the fulfillment of Cozzens's intent.

In diagramming the flow of power through a collectivity he has in no way committed himself to the thesis that the "historic" effect of that power on the Axis or on subsequent history is more significant or noteworthy than its effect on the individuals who were involved in its transmission. If anyone can extract from such representation the guidelines for political, cultural, or social reform, they will do so without specific encouragement from a writer who shows with such prodigal and hopeless patience how things were and are. He is among those who help us examine life without encouraging us either to judge it or to try to act upon it.

8

BERNARD DE VOTO

The Novelist as Professional[1]

For a long time I have pondered the status of Mr. Cozzens in official literary opinion and after reading his *Guard of Honor* I followed him, with the help of the periodical indexes, through the synoptic gospels of that opinion. When I finished I was not so much bewildered as shocked. Surely for at least eighteen years now—*S.S. San Pedro* was published eighteen years ago—it has been obvious that he has one of the finest talents and one of the most expert skills at work in American fiction. I say "surely" not merely because it has been obvious to me but because there is no one among my acquaintances, literary or lay, who does not feel as I do about his work. The writers whom I know (it is true that I am not intimate with any upper-caste literary critics) all think of him as one of our best novelists, one of our exceedingly few first-raters. That is less significant than the fact that, so far as my experience goes, the species of intelligent, discriminating people who regard fiction as a fine art, for whom fiction primarily exists, think the same. But, as the indexes reveal, Mr. Cozzens has had less attention from the formulators of official literary judgment than any other novelist of his rank and stature.

This fact is incongruous only on the surface. The explanation can be found in a remark that Mr. William Faulkner, also a novelist of the highest rank, recently made when an interviewer quoted to him some pidgin English intended to announce the discovery by a critic of qualities in Mr. Faulkner's work that he himself did not know were there. The critic had isolated from his new novel something that sounded like asymmetrical trivalent agglutinations of polyhedral tropes. Such a report would arrest any novelist's attention and Mr. Faulkner appears to have received it gravely but to have been unable to cope with it. He asked the interviewer's leave to be excused: something was wrong here, some mistake had been made, the words didn't apply to him. He was not, he said, a literary man: he was a writer.

That explains why criticism shies away from Mr. Cozzens: he is a writer. His novels are written. The word has to be italicized: they are *written*. So they leave criticism practically nothing to do. They are not born of a cause but of a fine novelist's feeling for the lives of people and for their destiny—so criticism cannot reproach him for not having made peace with Russia or praise him for having ended anti-Semitism in Coos County. They contain no fog of confused thinking on which, as on a screen, criticism can project its diagrams of meanings which the novelist did not know were there. There is in them no mass of unshaped emotion, the novelist's emotion or the characters', from which criticism can dredge up significance that becomes portentous as the critic calls our attention, and the novelist's, to it. Worse still, they are written with such justness that criticism cannot get a toehold to tell him and us how they should have been written. Worst of all, the novelist's ego has been disciplined out of them, so criticism cannot chant its dirge about the dilemmas of the artist in our time.

I do not know Mr. Cozzens but I am confident that he does not think of himself as the artist in our time or even as an artist. He is a professional. The word is an obscenity among those whom Mr. Faulkner called literary men but writers hold it in the highest respect. The professional as novelist is a man who has subdued himself to what he works in, who holds himself humbly in relation to fiction but holds fiction to be the most important thing in the world, whose deepest shame it would be not to write his novel wholly in the terms which the novel itself sets. He is also a man who has mastered his job and substitutes skill for literary pretensions and affectations. In his novels form and content are so welded together that they have become inseparable; they are the same thing. Moreover, each of his novels is a handful of novels made one; it is packed tight with life; any of its parts or characters and many of its mere parentheses would make a novel for a smaller man. There are single scenes in *Guard of Honor* that a second-rate novelist could blow up into a career.

Guard of Honor can be called a "war novel." The term makes little sense, as who should say a Methodist Episcopal Church South novel. Novels are about people and war is a set of circumstances that affect people, but if you say "war novel" you have established a category and so will comfort the questing mind. And the season has produced two other war novels that illuminate the preferences of truly literary thinking. Both give off the butyric perfume of sentimentality, which the highest order of criticism begins to admire as soon as it gets pretentious enough. One would have been a sound novel except that the author undertook to put the whole war into it and was not up to the job, so that it is thin and infinitely confused—and therefore, at the critic's will, rich with the portentous. The other is crammed with falsity and phoniness and pose and the literary view, and the novelist sticks out of it like a flagstaff, fastidious, hurt, and ah, God! how dismayed.

Guard of Honor is unfairly matched against the anemia, pretentious prose, inexpert management, and literary attitude of such books. In a few hundred pages it brings an enormous cast of characters so alive that they are not only true in the moment they are before our eyes but have compacted in its compass the experience that has made them what they are now and will be from now on. The novelist is not in the novel at all, except that when we have finished reading it we must reflect that only wisdom, a deep sense of reality, and great skill could have persuaded us to accept this fiction as the true thing. It wakens in us the grave tenderness we feel for the finalities of human experience, and it concentrates on those finalities, letting the literary thing and the novelist's soul go by the board. Of course the champs muffed it: it is not literary, it is not pretentious, it is a first-rate novel.

Quietly, with a sure hand and a purpose obviously untroubled by critical attitudes, Mr. Cozzens has been writing first-rate novels for a long time. The applause of deckle-edge thinkers has mostly been reserved for other kinds of novels, but no one who has ever read a novel of his has forgotten it. Apparently he has got to be content with the satisfaction of readers—the most sensitive and intelligent readers—and, for what it is worth, the admiration of writers. He will value the first much more than the second, and the preoccupation of official critical opinion with his inferiors cannot bother him at all. He is not a literary man, he is a writer. There are a handful like him in every age. Later on it turns out that they were the ones who wrote that age's literature.

9

JOHN FISCHER

Nomination for a Nobel Prize[1]

It now seems likely that the chief literary event of this year will be the discovery of James Gould Cozzens.

"Discovery" may seem an odd word to use about a man who has been writing for thirty-three years with unusual success, and who has been regarded by many people for at least a decade as one of the best American novelists. But no other word will do.

For Cozzens has never been fully recognized by two groups on which a lasting literary reputation depends: (a) the mass reading public, and (b) the serious critics. Both have largely ignored him— for a set of curious but understandable reasons. They can ignore him no longer. The publication this week of *By Love Possessed* makes him as hard to overlook as a giraffe in the living-room.

Although it is a violation of The Cozzens Security System to say so, this is his twelfth novel. Only eight are listed in the official roster of his works. His first four—*Confusion, Michael Scarlett, Cockpit,* and *Son of Perdition*—are never mentioned these days by him or his publisher, and their very existence is supposed to be a secret. Yet they are not books of which the average novelist would be ashamed, particularly in view of the circumstances under which they were produced. The first was written while he was a nineteen-year-old Harvard sophomore. When he found a publisher for it, in 1924, Cozzens decided he was in business, dropped out of college, and plunged immediately into the grinding and precarious labor of the professional novelist. On the next three books he learned his craft. He doesn't like to have them read now, for the same reason that

Yehudi Menuhin would not like to have a recording distributed of his early finger exercises—although one of them is a better-than-mine-run historical, and another, about a sorely-tempted priest, compares well enough with a famous Graham Greene novel on a similar theme.

(If you ever run across one of these early efforts in a second-hand bookstore, buy it. Since they are scarce, and almost sure to become collectors' items, they ought to turn out to be speculations at least as interesting as, say, General Dynamics or U. S. Borax.)

By ordinary standards, the next seven novels did well. They got respectful—sometimes enthusiastic—reviews. Three were chosen by the Book-of-the-Month Club, and all continued to sell far longer than the average novel. In fact, all but one are still in print—three in paperback editions—while the remaining one, *Men and Brethren,* will be brought back into print next year. To most novelists, whose books commonly disappear like a stone dropped in the sea about six months after publication, this looks like an enviable record.

Nevertheless, no Cozzens novel has ever become a really big seller. The last and best known—*Guard of Honor,* published in 1948—has sold about thirty thousand copies; compared with the marshmallows turned out by such wholesale confectioners as Frances Parkinson Keyes and Daphne du Maurier, its readership is tiny.

It is true that some other novelists of stature—William Faulkner, Glenway Wescott, Eudora Welty, and Thornton Wilder, for example—have seldom enjoyed enormous sales, and even Ernest Hemingway reached bestsellerdom fairly late. But they have been accorded other things most writers value even higher: literary prizes, the honors of the American Academy of Arts and Letters, and the reverence—indeed, the adulation—of the magisterial critics whose encyclicals appear in the literary quarterlies and academic journals. Aside from a Pulitzer Prize in 1949, no such laurels have lighted on Cozzens's head, and the fashionable critics have passed him by in contemptuous silence.

This time it may be different. Certain evanescent signs, which publishers think they can recognize, seem to indicate that *By Love Possessed* will sell far better than any previous Cozzens novel. The prepublication sale is high; booksellers, a notoriously glum lot, are betraying gleams of eagerness; it is a selection of both the Book-of-the-Month Club and Reader's Digest Condensed Books; review copies have been in heavy demand; *Time* is planning a cover story on the author; and—best omen of all—stenographers in the publishers office have been snitching advance copies to read during their lunch hour. When that happens, you can be sure that something uncommon is astir.

It would be no surprise, to this reader at least, if the new novel also collects a few prizes. At this writing, no very formidable contenders for the Pulitzer Prize and National Book Award can be spotted on the fall lists. (Although that may not mean much; in recent years each of these literary lollipops has been handed occasionally to a pretty feeble and precious specimen.)

And eventually even the most lordly of the academic critics may have to take judicial notice of Cozzens's existence. They won't like him; but from now on it will be hard for them to pretend that a man who occupies so much of the literary landscape simply isn't there.

They have preferred to ignore him all these years because he does not fit into any of the established literary patterns; and they have, therefore, found it impossible to measure and dissect him with their standard calipers and scalpels.

Even his private life is, for a writer, unconventional. He attends no cocktail parties, sits on no committees, makes no speeches, signs no manifestoes, writes no reviews, appears on no television shows, scratches no backs, shuns women's clubs, cares nothing about personal publicity, and doesn't even tell his publisher how to run his advertising campaigns. He holds the queer notion that a novelist's job is to write novels; and he sticks to that last with single-minded intensity. To this end, he lives and works in a quiet old farmhouse near Lambertville, New Jersey, with the only wife he has ever had (and who happens to be, quite incidentally, one of the best literary agents in the country); he almost never visits New York; few people in the so-called literary world have ever set eyes on him. Consequently he has picked up the reputation of a recluse.

It is undeserved. Actually he spends a good many sociable hours around Lambertsville and two neighboring towns, New Hope and Doylestown, Pennsylvania; and he is working every minute of them. He knows the Doylestown courthouse, for example, better than its janitor does, and its occupants—from judges to jailers—are his friends. It is no accident that the law, which figures largely in both this novel and an earlier one, is taken with precise accuracy from the Pennsylvania statutes; and that Brocton, the town which serves as a setting for the new novel, bears a family resemblance to the villages along the middle stretch of the Delaware River.

The graph line of Cozzens's career also looks remarkably different from that of many American novelists. As the literary historians have noted, talented writers in this country often start off with a bang, and then dwindle away to a whimper. Sinclair Lewis, for instance, ran steadily downhill after he reached his early high point with *Main Street* and *Babbitt.* Thomas Wolfe never again wrote anything quite up to his first novel, *Look Homeward, Angel.* Even Faulkner and Hemingway have followed much the same chart. Faulkner's most bedazzled admirers would hardly claim that his last two books are up to the level of his earlier work, and Hemingway's most recent novel, *Across the River and Into the Trees,* is best passed over in charitable silence. (A subsequent book, *The Old Man and the Sea,* is a long short story rather than a novel.) A list of similar examples could be continued for pages; but Cozzens would not be on it. His output has shown a steady growth in sureness, insight, and stature, so that the present monumental work comes not as a surprise but as a natural culmination.

These are relatively superficial differences. The essential difference between Cozzens and his contemporaries lies in the character of his work. Here he is the complete nonconformist: a classic mind, operating in a romantic period. This, I suspect, is the basic reason why he has missed both popular and critical appreciation. He puzzles ordinary readers whose palates have been dulled by the Gothic extravagance of most current fiction; and he offends critics whose professional mission has been to exalt the romantic novel which has been in high fashion for the last thirty years.

The Standard American Romantic novelist of today can be identified by four earmarks:

(1) He habitually writes about exotic characters who are, in one fashion or another, in revolt against society. Witness Faulkner's Popeye and Joe Christmas, Steinbeck's lovable bums, Hemingway's defiant tough guys, Tennessee Williams's prostitutes and heels, Capote's Southerners, Saroyan's elfin drunks, and all the other dope addicts, cheats, thieves, goldbricks, and emotional cripples who are the stock in trade of Nelson Algren, Norman Mailer, Saul Bellow, Paul Bowles, James Jones, and the other inhabitants of our contemporary Pantheon.

(2) He conventionally portrays such heroes in sentimental terms—as Edmund Fuller pointed out in last spring's issue of the *American Scholar.* "It is not my hero's fault," the romantic novelist tells us, "that he is an irresponsible jerk. Society made him that way." And he invites the reader to drop a kindly tear for these scala-

wags—what Fuller calls "the genial rapist, the jolly slasher, the fun-loving dope pusher"—just as the sentimental novelist of the last century asked us to weep over his forlorn maidens.

(3) Usually, though not always, he places his picaresque heroes in a picaresque tale. Such a story need have no firm plot structure; it wanders haphazardly from one incident to another, linking anecdotes, sketches, short stories, and inner musings together with a loose and tenuous narrative line. Its setting is often as exotic as the characters—the Chicago underworld, a rum runner's boat, a bull ring, Yoknapatawpha County—and the story ordinarily involves a wholesale helping of lust and violence.

(4) The novelist of this school customarily identifies himself with one of his characters and uses him as a trumpet to express his own emotions, complaints, and political views. Sometimes (as in Wolfe) the hero is the spitting image of the author; sometimes (as in Hemingway, the highbrow's Walter Mitty) he seems to be the way the author pictures himself in his more glorious day-dreams; sometimes (as in Steinbeck and Algren) he is the ventriloquist's dummy on the author's knee. In any case, it is easy to tell which speeches in the book set forth the author's sermon; Faulkner leaves no doubt where he stands in the War Against the Snopeses.

There is much to be said for the romantic method. For one thing, it is the easiest way to catch the interest of the reader—typically a man or woman who leads a sedentary, respectable, uneventful life, and therefore is ready to shiver with excitement at the wild doings of the uninhibited outlaw. It is a time-saver, since the picaresque plot is no trouble to construct; some of its practitioners turn out a book a year. It is a simple and effective device for criticizing society—always a main purpose of the novelist in America. And it is a boon to the critic, since it gives him a built-in springboard from which to launch his own dissertation about the society we live in.

But the romantic novel has its drawbacks, too. Because it uses the extreme case—abnormal characters in an abnormal setting—as a weapon to attack the evils that exist in all societies, it can never give a full and balanced picture of society as a whole. A foreigner can (and often does) read a hundred such novels without getting the faintest ideas of what normal, day-to-day life in the United States is really like. Falukner's guilt-haunted county and Algren's vice-pots may give accurate glimpses of tiny segments on the extreme fringe of American life—and it is, of course, useful to put these pathological specimens under the microscope. But they do not picture the rounded body of society, any more than L. F. Céline's explorations of depravity reflect the whole truth about contemporary France.

Then, too, the sentimental stance of this sort of fiction—handy though it is for posing an indictment of society—makes it impossible for the writer to deal seriously with individual moral problems. *From Here to Eternity,* for example, made it plain that plenty was wrong with the prewar Army; but at the cost of evading all questions about the personal responsibilities of Prewitt, who had to be pictured as a helpless victim of The System. In all such novels—*The Deer Park* and *The Man with the Golden Arm* are even better examples—one vital dimension of fiction necessarily is missing.

Finally, the romantic method tends to wear itself out in a few decades. Readers get jaded with lust and violence and bizarre heroes; to hold their attention, the novelist has to reach for ever greater extremes; and in the end his readers cease to believe in characters so remote from their own experience. The resulting boredom and indifference are perhaps largely responsible for the much-discussed decline of fiction. Maybe the romantic novel has, for a time, reached a dead end.

Cozzens may, indeed, signal a turning of the tide. In his salad days, he too flirted with the romantic technique, but in his mature novels he has moved steadily away from it. Instead he has been attempting something far more difficult: to write an engrossing story about ordinary people, living ordinary lives, in ordinary circumstances.

His first experiment in this direction was *The Last Adam,* published in 1933, an account of a small-town doctor and his patients. *Men and Brethren* dealt with the life of a New York clergyman, not very different from the parson you might meet next Sunday. *The Just and the Unjust* was a study of law and politics in a perfectly commonplace community. *Guard of Honor* examined life on a Florida air base in all its levels and complexities; anyone who served in World War II would feel at home there, but he would encounter none of the grotesque characters who man the Armies of Jones and Mailer. (It may be significant that many professional military men consider it the best of the war novels; one Air Force colonel told me it was the *only* one that showed any awareness of the actual problems of Army life.)

By Love Possessed carries this series of experiments-in-the-normal a long and brilliant step forward. On all four of the counts listed above, it is the exact antithesis of the romantic novel.

Its central characters are a group of lawyers and businessmen—

middle-class, middle-aged, and respectable—in an American town no better and no worse than a dozen any of us could name. They move among people familiar to all of us: a spinster secretary, a justice of the peace, a waitress, an overworked doctor, an assortment of immediately recognizable wives and children. Nobody is presented as a rebel against society, or as its victim; these people *are* society. When they try to rebel, it is not against The System, but against life itself, and they fall victim to the mortality that awaits us all.

Of sentimentality there is no chemical trace. You are never asked to weep for any character, or to rage. You are merely invited to understand them, as the author probes deeper and deeper for the final meaning in each of their lives. What he finds is not always pretty, but neither is it monstrous. It comes close to being the truth, the whole truth, and nothing but the truth, so help me God.

This is no loose-woven picaresque tale. It is the most tightly-constructed of novels, with every chapter—indeed, every paragraph—carved to interlock with every other. In the end it emerges as a work of classic symmetry—the last scene foreshadowed in the first, all parts in balance, all conflicts resolved. The style is equally craftsmanlike. Every sentence has been hammered, filed, and tested until it bears precisely the weight it was designed to carry, and does it with clarity and grace. No wonder this book took nine years to write.

Not once does the author himself walk into the story. No character is autobiographical, none is a loudspeaker for the author's sermons. When you finish you know a lot about Cozzens's concept of the good life—but only because you have watched a number of lives unfold in vigorous detail before your eyes.

The theme of the book is love. Love in all its aspects—between man and woman, parent and child, friend and friend, individual and community. It is an examination of the rewards and the burdens—sometimes crushing burdens—laid on people possessed by love. And like all really first-rate novels, it is an exploration of moral responsibility. Each person who inhabits the story is constantly confronted (though he does not always realize it) with the series of moral questions which confront all of us: How should I conduct myself? What is my duty? Can I escape this hard choice before me? What do I do next?

It is a measure of Cozzens's accomplishment that he endows such a story with a feeling of suspense and excitement far greater than you will find in the typical romantic novel, loaded with violent action.

The explanation, it seems to me, it that the ordinary reader can identify himself with the people of Brocton, as he never can with the characters of an Algren or a Mailer. The dilemma Arthur Winner faces, as he sits in his tidy law office, is one any of us might encounter tomorrow. The temptation that brought Ralph Detweiler into the hands of the police and his sister to her death is commonplace in every village in America. Never for a moment can you doubt these are real people, coping with real problems in the fumbling, unromantic way that all of us try to cope with our own.

To be fair, it is necessary to note two complaints about the book:

(1) Several women, of sound taste and judgment, tell me that they find the story disconcerting. They are not used to seeing love handled in such an unsentimental fashion, and they are not sure they like it. Moreover, I gather that they are a little upset by the fact that the issue on which the novel hinges does not involve a woman at all. It centers on the spiritual love of a patriarch for the people who have trusted him (perhaps too much) and on a question of professional ethics. Now most mature women realize, in their hearts, that the chief crises in a man's life may have nothing to do with females; but they don't always like to be reminded of it. The romantic legend— older than Helen of Troy—that a woman is the central core of every man's life, the focus of his worries, and the mainspring of his actions, is more soothing to the feminine ego.

(2) Other people, by no means prudes, have suggested that *By Love Possessed* is not a suitable book for the young. They may be right. It was, after all, written for adults; and some of its passages might well be both incomprehensible and disturbing to adolescents who lack the range of experience to grasp the emotions involved.

This is not to suggest that anything in the story is either salacious or sensational. Quite the contrary. Cozzens has merely tried to tell the exact truth—about sex, money, ambition, and many other things—with clinical honesty. Some aspects of the truth inevitably are unpleasant. These he has neither softened nor exaggerated. They are set down with the raw, impersonal horror of an autopsy or a police report, because they are a part of life; so, too, are warmth and devotion and quiet heroism, and these he reports with equal fidelity.

The novel is like one of those Breughel paintings that show an entire community in bustling activity—the noble, the funny, the bestial, the labor and lust, the pain and laughter, all traced out in infinitely precise detail . . . and all the details fitted together to form a marvelously colorful composition. Like Breughel, Cozzens tells us more than any artist of his time about the life of his day. If your great-grandchild should ever want to find out how Ameicans behaved and thought and felt in the mid-years of this century. Cozzens's major novels probably would be his most revealing source.

If this does not stake out his claim to be one of the very few important novelists of our generation, I don't know what would. The committee that awards the Nobel prize for literature is said to reach its decisions, not on the basis of a single book, but on mature consideration of a writer's whole body of work. Where can they find a more solid body of work than this?

10

LELAND H. COX, JR.

Henry Dodd Worthington:
The "I" in *Morning Noon and Night*

With the opening lines of *Morning Noon and Night,* Henry Dodd Worthington, the novel's narrator and central character, makes a statement of fact: "I have been young and now am old."[1] Throughout the remainder of the text, Worthington—who is now past sixty and is the president of his own highly prestigious mangement-consultant firm—undertakes to render his personal version of the life he has led and to state what, if anything, he has learned from it. This is an act that immediately sets him apart from the central characters in Cozzens's previous twelve novels; for Worthington is the first mature central character in Cozzens's fiction to assume the role of first-person narrator. Unlike his most immediate counterparts—Arthur Winner *(By Love Possessed)* and Judge Ross *(Guard of Honor)*—Worthington has the advantage of being able to talk directly about himself.[2] He is therefore in a superb position to explore in personal and minute detail what Louis Coxe calls "the double vision of modern man, the central paradox of action and contemplation, of understanding and conduct, of the ironic view and the heroic efficacy"[3] that characterizes Cozzens's best writing. Henry Worthington, speaking of himself and others, speaks profoundly on the nature of experience and self-knowledge: on the variegated existence of man as a responsible member of society, as a tough-minded professional, and even as a creative individual.

This view by no means represents the consensus of the few critics who have commented on *Morning Noon and Night.* Most have maintained—in what has become something of a cliché in the Cozzens field—that in this his thirteenth novel Cozzens simply persisted in using the medium of fiction as a channel through which he advances his own conservative views into the light of common day; that in the character of Henry Dodd Worthington we have nothing less (or more) than the official mouthpiece of James Gould Cozzens.[4] It does not take a particularly close reading of *Morning Noon and Night,* or of any other Cozzens novel, to dispel this sort of nonsense. I mention it here to illustrate a single point: that most of the critics who attack Cozzens and his craft with greatest vehemence do so because they persist in imposing a simplistic view onto fictional characters and situations of great complexity and subtlety. They fail to criticize Cozzens's fiction on its own terms.

It is precisely because Henry Worthington is not able to find a simple formula that will give order and coherence to his past life that he labors so mightily to compose his recollection of it. Trying to answer the most enigmatic of questions (*"What is this life? Who am I; what is this 'I' in me?"* [p. 5]), he is deeply troubled by what he describes as "a loss of sureness, with which growing old increasingly afflicts me and, I suspect, all men by temperament given to reflection. Opinions of mine, once quite settled, tend more and more of them to become unsettled. . . . However improved [by being occasionally disabused of old biases], the mind has also been caused to stand again and again painfully corrected, letting the lurking principle of uncertainty insinuate itself" (p. 5). Not only because he is contemplative by nature, but also because he has a first-rate mind, Worthington is quick to recognize many of the misconceptions, errors of logic, and simple foibles of human nature that might otherwise stand between him and the accurate perception of possible causes and effects in his own life and in the lives of those who are closest to him. Uncertainty does not produce a condition of intellectual or physical paralysis because of Worthington's own healthy skepticism, a quality very similar to what he detects in his father as having been "a sort of silent patient withholding of judgment" (p. 287). A contemplative skeptic—who is nevertheless capable of acting in the face of uncertainty—Henry Worthington must draw his data from the wellsprings of personal experience as he attempts to come to terms with what his life has been; and that inevitably turns him back to viewing himself almost simultaneously in the varied contexts of personal and professional relationships that can be recalled to the level of consciousness.

Since he cannot relive his life, Henry Worthington must rely on memory as his only available tool in re-creating past roles and relationships, and in analyzing past experiences. This in itself is something of a problem, for Worthington has played many roles. In the sixty-odd years of his existence he has been student, husband, lover, father, bill collector, military officer, would-be-writer, and—for some time now—presiding officer of his own consulting firm. Compounding the difficulty of evaluating these and other roles, and the experiences associated with them, is the unreliability of memory itself. It is eclectic, and Worthington realizes full well that a seemingly "bad" memory might actually be the work of a psychological defense mechanism, helpfully impairing one's ability to remember unpleasant events. It is also impossible to trust memory as "that warder of the brain charged with receipt of reason; or a file of stored-away sense impressions; or a compendium of ideas entertained; or a lexicon, well or ill compiled, of experience's teaching; or an unplanned, unindexed commonplace book; or a mechanically kept chronicle, a historical record . . . of past events, of things gone but . . . not forgotten" (pp. 11–12). The workings of memory are simply too diffuse and selective to be systematically ordered. Moreover, Worthington recognizes the contradiction that exists between the way he has trained his mind to work and the essentially untrainable vagaries of memory: "My mind is so constituted that in its everyday exercises it likes, even craves, order. A plodder, my mind would prefer to begin at beginnings, proceed through unfolding middles, and end with endings. My memory seems not to be so constituted. Give it liberty, and order be damned; and since I am only limited master or director, liberty it takes, it has" (p. 67). Thus what the real nature of memory might be is no easier to understand "than the nature of electricity. The one, like the other, comes to be comprehended only in what it does, how it acts" (p. 11). Though inconclusive as to how memory ought to be regarded or dealt with, Worthington's early recapitulation of what is for him a nagging problem is of extreme importance. He can maintain with reasonable credibility that, like the Psalmist of old, what he has "to say about life deserves attention" (p. 3), and that he and the Psalmist, having become wise by growing old, "ought to be, as well as heard, heeded" (p. 3). On the other hand, what Worthington goes on to say about himself and life in general should not be accepted blindly by those comprising his audience. Given the various caveats that are provided concerning the nature of memory, we should meet each of the narrator's statements and conclusions with a question suggested by

Worthington himself: *"Who, what manner of man, says so?"* (p. 33).
How, then, does Henry Worthington proceed, and what does he
actually make of the life he has led?

Worthington's narrative is carried along chiefly by a process of
association of ideas. Remembering a conversation with his daughter
Elaine concerning her several marital and sexual problems, Worthington is led to reflect on how his own notions of sexuality have
changed. This in turn causes him to think of his family background
and leads eventually to a brief treatise—having to do with Worthington's maternal grandfather, Professor Ethelbert Cuthbertson
("Cubby") Dodd—on how sheer coincidence can set in motion a
chain of circumstances that ultimately produce a living and virtually
unshakeable legend about Professor Dodd that is founded not in the
least on his own scholarly merits, which are quite modest. Memory
comes full circle as Worthington's mind is called back to the original
interview with Elaine. Here Elaine's disclosure to her father of her
early sexual awakening—the catalyst for which was Elaine's discovery, at the age of fourteen, of her mother's promiscuity—evokes
in Worthington the memory of his own introduction to sex by an
older woman.

It is in this seemingly unstructured fashion that Henry Worthington moves through his recollections of the various roles he has
played; and indeed, the process of narration corresponds with what
Worthington has had to say earlier about the inconsistencies inher-
ent in memory's operation. To discover how it is that Worthington
evaluates his life, and what he thinks of the way he has lived it, I
would like to concentrate on two particular aspects of the narration:
(1) the personal relationships of Henry Worthington with women
(his daughter Elaine, Mrs. Eunice Van den Arend—the woman who
introduced him to sex—and his two wives, Judith and Charlotte);
and (2) Worthington's comments on the craft of writing. Together,
Henry Worthington's views on sex and art reveal much about himself and the structure of his autobiography.

It is Elaine who occupies the central position among the women of
Worthington's life. His own sexual awakening was similar to hers,
and, as indicated above, it is Elaine who sparks the chain of mental
association that leads to various analyses of sex, love, and marriage.
Cozzens's presentation of setting and character combine for an
ironic introduction to Elaine. When we first see her, she is in her
father's office lamenting her marital failures. Over thirty, she has
been divorced twice and her third marriage seems headed for the

rocks. In a novel that stresses the importance of good management in one's personal and professional life, Elaine appears almost totally inept. By speaking of marriage as an explicit exchange of rights and privileges, she shows a basic misunderstanding of the relationship. "As I saw it," she says, "in exchange for my marrying him [Wilfred, her first husband] he was always supposed to do what I wanted. That was the deal. I was going to let him lay me ad lib. He was going to be my humble servant" (p. 74). One month after her first divorce, Elaine decides to remarry and carries off the enterprise with all the precision of a soundly organized business campaign: "adding up all things to the good, I cast the die; and now to business" (p. 80). For Worthington's daughter, cynicism is a defensive mechanism that only serves to muddle her thinking; for the cynic is leading invariably from a weak hand, and although Worthington's outlook on life has its skeptical aspects, it never becomes a masque for self-pity.

Elaine's problem is really psychological, and she has developed a talent for conveniently forgetting what she doesn't want to remember. Sharing her father's penchant for self-analysis, she lacks his rational objectivity; and her judgments are frequently distorted by excessive emotionalism. Elaine serves then as a kind of foil to her father, her own character and habits of mind—despite some general similarities—showing the reverse side of his. This is seen especially in the ways that Elaine reacts to the events in her life that have had some psychological impact, the earliest of which was her introduction at an early age to the world of adult, and adulterous, sex. The event takes place at Old Harbor, a resort where Worthington owns a summer home he has inherited from his father. The shock of discovery hinges upon the chance that Elaine, walking among the dunes on the beach, accidentally observes her mother having sexual intercourse with one of her father's clients. As a young girl Elaine had " 'never been quite sure what men did with women. I suppose,' " she tells her father, " 'I was horrified. In fact, I know I was. More even by *that*, I think, than by its being mother' " (pp. 157–58). Elaine's disclaimer concerning the psychological impact of the event is questionable. " 'Sure,' " she reasons, " 'in books you read about that kind of shock being terribly traumatic—an adolescent's supposed never to get over it. But I'll bet, when that happens, the brat was all along a damn odd brat' " (p. 159). Presumably, Elaine does not see herself as an "odd brat"; yet almost twenty years after her experience at Old Harbor, she has been unable to establish a meaningful sexual relationship with any of her three husbands. And her inability to come to grips with the reasons for her mother's behavior is a persistent source of emotional anguish. Elaine is beset by doubts, and at times feels that her mother " 'wished she hadn't had me' " (p. 209). Years later, when Judith is in the late stages of terminal illness, Elaine tells her father, " 'You see, I really don't like Mother a bit. And now look at her' " (p. 203).

Worthington's insight into his daughter's problems is self-revealing. He is not so much disappointed in Elaine as he is disturbed over her misfortunes. "If an Elaine," he reasons, "abstinent and ascetic, avoids doing or helping to do a job of disfigurement on herself, in the long run will time fail to do one indistinguishable from it on her anyway?" (p. 72). In no way does Worthington indicate that he considers himself to be a failure as a parent; and his concern for Elaine's welfare seems to be genuine. What his behavior reveals primarily is a dispassionate and consistent belief that he cannot step in and lead her life for her, any more so than he could when Judith, his first wife, once expressed concern over the possibility that Elaine, who was in college at the time, might be having an affair. Worthington remembers having replied that " 'If it's true you can't do anything; if it isn't true nothing needs to be done' " (p. 75). This kind of pronouncement serves two purposes. It tells us how Worthington—reaching back into memory's storehouse and recalling the garden interview, which by a process of association leads to a remembering of even earlier events in Elaine's growing up—sees himself as a parent, and what he conceives, regardless of Elaine's personal situation, some of the general principles of the human condition to be. One of the most important of these principles is that human beings will generally do what they want, even if the attainment of desire's goal makes them miserable; and that no amount of interference, well-intentioned or otherwise, will stand in their way. In Worthington's world, being the keeper of one's brother or daughter is simply an impossible task.

Reflections induced by Elaine's misunderstanding of love provide further insights into Worthington's character and his concept of relative values, the chief element of which is Time. The images of lust Elaine evokes are repugnant to her father not because they affront his moral sensibilities but because inappetency has come to him with age. But in his youth Worthington had no clear idea of the balance between love and sex. Is it the "listless prudery," the "faint malaise of disrelish," the "settled inappetency" (p. 90) of old age that labels love as mere sex? Or does youth mistakenly label sex as pure love? Worthington has the "double vision" necessary to penetrate both points of view: "To pantaloon nearing impotence, screwing is all that loving is. So be it; but for yesterday what screwing had been was heart of loving's heart. Repellent factual truths of love's bouts never were absent, but they hid themselves under fruitions for young Henry as food to life or as sweet seasoned showers are to the ground" (p. 94).

The scene of sexual initiation is the same for father and daughter. Worthington ("Young Hank" then) is not quite sixteen when he undertakes the role of lover, and the nature of his experience is even more dramatic than Elaine's. Worthington is on summer vacation at Old Harbor and is in the habit of encountering Eunice Van den Arend on the beach. Reflecting on the event Worthington analyzes the motivations involved in a manner that humorously undercuts the degree of prestige that might be attributed to adolescent sexual conquests. Hank savors his meetings with Mrs. Van den Arend as an opportunity for showing off in front of an older woman, "to impress her with what a lot he has read, and to make her admire his literary taste and cultural acumen" (p. 166). The older Henry can see that beneath these youthful pretensions was "a sudden discovery . . . that Eunice Van den Arend was a very attractive woman" (p. 166).

Just as Elaine is unable to offer an explanation for her mother's adultery, so Hank cannot readily understand Mrs. Van den Arend's willingness to commit adultery. As adolescents they are similar in their ignorance of sex: "What practical knowledge you came by . . . went no further than a knowing of the thing that happened. You beheld an effect but you were made no wiser about causes that could produce it, might explain it. If our Hank on his afternoon knew more than Elaine knew on hers about copulation, he knew it only in the bare terms of the physical or anatomical" (p. 170). As was the case with Elaine, Hank's first sexual experience produces an initial shock. What remains a dormant urge, or dream, or wish fulfillment for most adolescent males faces Hank as a reality.

If Hank can conceive no rational explanation for Mrs. Van den Arend's behavior ("A dream girl his mind created might do as Mrs. Van den Arend has done" [p. 180], he at least has latent in him the temperament that later enables Henry Worthington to posit a logical cause. Worthington rejects images of Mrs. Van den Arend as a woman whose sexual appetites are not sufficiently satisfied, or as a pervert "to whom the scared neophyte is not better than nothing but better than anything" (p. 180). For Mrs. Van den Arend, Hank is simply a tool of revenge to be used against her husband, a man of amazing virility who cannot be satisfied by one woman. It is not mere chance that works Hank's seduction. He represents the culmination of a cycle of cause and effect, and Mrs. Van den Arend can count on fear to keep him quiet. Of course, the positing of this cause-and-effect relationship is purely hypothetical on Worthington's part. The attributes and motivations of Mrs. Van den Arend are given as suppositions, not proven facts. Once more, Henry Worthington reveals what is for him an underlying principle of thought and action. The principle of thought is the good sense latent in systematically seeking out an hypothesis that answers more questions than it leaves unanswered. Such a process can never be guaranteed to supply anyone with conclusive proof about any human condition. It can, however, provide a reasonable basis upon which one might choose to act. In most of his personal and professional relationships, Henry Worthington has embraced this principle consistently. Thus we should be inclined to accept Worthington's explanation of Mrs. Van den Arend's behavior as being plausible. What we must also keep in mind is that, at the time, Young Hank was completely incapable of performing such a rational feat. The kind of experience he is subjected to—"the boy brought for the first time to attempt the man's work is as good as bound to botch it badly. . . . Since he was male, proof of how little a man he was would be likely to seem to him a crushing shame, a disgrace forever" (p. 185)—is one that the older Worthington is able to view dispassionately and suggest reasons for only in retrospect. His ability to do so is consistent with and supports Elaine's earlier judgment: "traumata of the sort will usually prove in the long run to be only flesh wounds" (p. 179).

The concept of marriage as a "deal" (first argued by Elaine and denied by Worthington) reveals another side of the narrator's character. "I would be curious to know," thinks Worthington, "just when Judith reached a firm decision to marry me. I wouldn't then have been able to tell because in those days it never occurred to me that the deciding wasn't to be mine. I never knew that virtually all marriages are arranged by the woman" (pp. 270–71). What Worthington denies to his daughter he admits to himself: "The thoughtful good sense shown, the provident wish (whose sound principle is: *nothing for nothing and very little for sixpence*) to act circumspectly strike me as much to the credit of feminine nature, sometimes stigmatized as uncertain, coy, and hard to please. That women don't as a rule allow idiot compulsions of True Love, either the besottedly romantic sort, or the carnal screw-we-must sort, to make fools of them I think praiseworthy." (p. 271). Such factual analysis may have general validity, but it only obscures (perhaps intentionally) the real motivations behind the marriage of Judith Conway and Henry Worthington. Judith wishes to carry on her revolt against her father, and Henry sees an opportunity for almost unlimited pleasures that are free for the asking: "When day in day out Judith will make these his for the asking, how could he, why should he, doubt even a moment that he'll be loving her always?" (p. 94).

Analyses made by Worthington of his second marriage reveal still more of his character. As Judith is antipathetic to any father image, so Charlotte is dependent totally upon one. Worthington takes the fact that Charlotte's first husband was old enough to have been her father as the starting point for his analysis: "Of course the significance I spoke of now being able to see [the age of Charlotte's first husband] was just that. Charlotte, out of known or unknown emotional need, married him because he was old enough to be her father, because presumably he could represent for her some sort of father image into whose hands she would happily render herself" (p. 368). Earlier in the novel Elaine, cynically degrading her sexual motivations, tells her father that " 'All that's in me is I crave a roll in the hay. If I happen to be wanting it bad, maybe it's a little like: I have to have him—no choice [which is how Worthington tried to explain her mother's behavior to her]. But still, I'm making one, aren't I?' " In reply Worthington tells Elaine that " 'people never choose to do what they don't want to do. What they do may be painful, disagreeable, very hard on them, but even so they plainly like doing it better than not doing it' " (p. 212). It follows that when Worthington takes a sexual interest in Charlotte he is acting in accordance with the above principle. Exploiting the one weakness in Charlotte that will preclude the possibility of refusal, Worthington's motivation is clear— "she will, all loving handmaidenly meekness . . . acquiesce, go in, undress, and lie down with him if she finds that what Father, dear Father, wants is to copulate with her" (p. 394). An ironic echo of the business metaphor that runs through the novel is heard when Worthington speaks of making Charlotte a partner in his firm. Instead Charlotte becomes a partner in marriage. When Worthington is unable to fulfill his contract as a father surrogate, his wife, withdrawing deeper into her depressed mind, puts a shotgun to her head. Later, and apparently with no feelings of guilt or responsibility, Worthington quotes Charlotte's suicide note and thereby reveals that it was he who inadvertently suggested the means to be employed: *"Hank . . . I just have to get out of this. I don't know why . . . I suppose it's bound to be messy and I'm sorry. But I keep remembering your saying once about somebody who tried but they saved him that if you really meant it you ought to do it like this. You said: then you're sure. Love. Charlotte"* (p. 216). In their respective marriages, both Henry Worthington and his daughter Elaine have experienced an uncommon amount of pain and anguish. It is significant, though, that Worthington is able to step outside of himself and objectify his marital experiences, while Elaine indulges her guilt feelings through self-condemnation and self-pity.

Henry Worthington's objectivity gives him the ability to reveal incisively the strengths and weaknesses of other people, and throughout *Morning Noon and Night* his analytical eye is turned on himself as well as others. One of the areas in which objective self-criticism is the most important is in Henry Worthington's comments on the craft of writing; for, as the author of his personal memoirs, he at times plays the twin roles of writer and critic. His first comments on writing are given in connection with his early ambition to be a professional writer, an ambition that waned rapidly following the "discovery that the work of writing can be easy only for those who haven't yet learned to write" (p. 59). Remembering this early discouragement, which was primarily a product of laziness, Worthington reflects on the attributes that must characterize the true professional:

> I think my giving up may of itself be good evidence that it was never in me to become a writer. I am prepared to believe that the life term at hard labor of serious writing, the disappointments of normal early failure . . . the active large and small nastinesses of the undercover melee, the slings and arrows of enemy criticism's addictive lying, and the poor financial pickings that are the average professional's ordinary lot can none of them, or all of them together, nonplus in the least a person with the true urge to write, the writer born. (pp. 59–60)

It is tempting to listen for the voice of Cozzens himself in these pronouncements, especially considering the abundant evidence of the "writer born" that is found in Cozzens's own fiction; and in his consistent ignoring of the literary moguls of his world Cozzens attracted more than his fair share of adverse criticism. In his writing about writing, however, Cozzens is not engaging in any "tendentious dialectics" (p. 244). He is instead writing about those aspects of life and work that he knows best, and it is for that reason that the "literary" portions of Henry Worthington's narration carry such a deep ring of conviction. It is indeed to Cozzens's credit that he is able to make Worthington's pronouncements such a central and effective aspect of the novel without, at the same time, making a straw man of his central character. Adroitly, Cozzens has Worthington tell us that he himself is not the kind of writer he professes to admire. What he and his creator have in common is the belief that the writer who writes truthfully of others must also be possessed of a strong measure of self-knowledge, and that the strength of his vision must transcend temporary difficulties such as occasional failure, muddle-headed or vindictive critics, or slight financial reward. The qualities of endurance, discipline, and singleness of purpose are precisely the ones that Worthington claims were not his; so he is not setting up any unfair comparison between himself and other would-be writers. It is still the function of the first-person narration to examine the motivating principles of human nature, but the focus has shifted from the area of Worthington's personal life into the world of professional letters.

Perhaps Worthington's most important early exposure to the world of letters—and literary people—was his attendance at a writers' conference with his Harvard classmate Knox Frothingham in the summer after their graduation:

> He notices the very noticeable fact . . . that a number of those present fall almost generically into types—the lank and flat-chested women's-college liberal, looking rather unwashed and rather debauched; the pompous, obstinately humorless revolutionary young man sprouting his bit of beard, yet in his nervous giggle less than virile; the craggy-faced, homespun, virile-indeed buck-fairy on his prowl for boy-does. . . . Even a few such look-and-act-alikes viewed grouped together can suggest an imitating, a copying of each other—which can in turn suggest (maybe not always fairly) that these are pretenders pretending; fakes, not real writing writers. (p. 247)

Worthington had gone to the conference supposing that "how to write was what they would study and discuss" (p. 243). Recalling that topics having to do with writing or literature were seldom touched upon, the elder Worthington views the early conference as an omen of things to come, of a "pretentiously named American Writers

Congress" that "would be centering its whole attention on how an abstract entity known as 'The Writer' ought to regard multitudinous intellectual 'issues' with which modern times supposedly confronted him" (p. 243). Worthington continues:

> Such full-blown solemn-asininity lay in the future; yet first winds of it, perplexing, question-raising, trouble a little the earlier intellectual symposium's calm. A butyric whiff of riper phoniness to come taints ever so faintly the rare atmosphere. Time had not been yet for main business to turn altogether from writing and become 'issues' and 'problems'; yet a number of the leaders and not a few of the led seemed . . . interested more in sounding off on the innocence of Sacco and Vanzetti than in the techniques of writing truthfully and exactly about life and people. (p. 244)

Acid sharp, Worthington's criticisms never reach the level of pure invective, primarily because he returns to examine what should be the professional writer's abiding concern: the presentation of the strengths and foibles of human nature. This concern is implicit in Worthington's almost dumbfounded question, "Didn't Doctor Johnson say: *Nothing can please many, or please long, but just representations of human nature?* (p. 244).[5]

Worthington's critical eye turns inward as well. Concerning his easy (and quite superficial) classification of "types" at the conference he attended, he reasons: "The show of even a few of their stamp may be judged to speak disturbingly to subliminal doubts of his about his own talent, about whether he, either, has it in him to be a real writer. Is he finding, through watching these people, himself exposed to himself?" (p. 248). Observing the same people and the same phenomena, Worthington's friend Knox—who does have the temperament of a real writer—reacts altogether differently: "Egotistically sanguine and confident, he watches them with contempt, sees them as simply good for unkind laughs; and once he is sure that staying in their company offers nothing from which he can profit, nothing to his writing purpose, he drops out" (p. 249).

The point of view from which Henry Worthington's comments on writing are delivered is also important. As he does in other sections of *Morning Noon and Night,* Cozzens shifts the narrative voice of his speaker and has Worthington refer to himself as "our Hank," "he," "him," or "himself." Shifts in point of view contribute to the narrative complexity of the novel and also help to delineate Worthington's character. The first of these changes is found almost at the beginning, when Worthington postulates a description of his own conception and birth, and a similar shift occurs in the telling of his experience with Mrs. Van den Arend, where Worthington refers to himself as "the watcher of the play" (p. 181). Though all of Cozzens's previous novels are written from the third person point of view, he found the first person voice better suited to his purposes in *Morning Noon and Night.* Used as sparingly as it is, the third person voice is extremely effective. Especially here, in the ten-page segment (pp. 241–50) where Worthington talks about his and Knox's attendance at a writer's conference, it creates an impression of extreme objectivity. It is this narrative objectivity that gives emphasis to the most important aspect of Worthington's character: his ability to stand outside of himself and (in this case) to view dispassionately the aspirations and assumptions—including his own—of real and would-be writers. His high degree of personal objectivity helps to make his comments on literature and writing not just plausible but credible. As we are enjoined to do at the beginning of the novel, we should be inclined to heed as well as hear what Henry Worthington has to say (p. 3).

Worthington's final comments on writing appear in the "Epilogue" to *Morning Noon and Night.* He first states his reasons for avoiding conventional narration: "I made the choice because I for long have felt that setting out courses of events in the natural, seemingly straightforward way can, oddly enough, distort truth and obscure meaning, at least in the sense of limiting or lessening for a reader his possible new acquist of true experience, since he will not have been told beforehand what he has to know if he is to grasp the real significance in many reported happenings" (p. 400). By imposing an unnatural order on the natural disorder of events, Worthington believes that the results would be the same kind of unbelievability "found in statements or confessions recorded by police stenographers" (p. 400). His point is simple and direct: the writer must seek—as Worthington does in his memoirs—the form that is most conducive to the telling of whatever truth is in him, and "problems of telling the truth are of sorest perplexity to every writer whose serious aim is a just representation of life and people" (p. 401). The means to this end are almost infinite, and Worthington maintains that ironclad formulae are not to be found either in the field of experimental writing or in the relatively simple and more conservative mode of traditional narration (p. 402).

It may be asked fairly, what is the reason for these lengthy comments on writers and writing, and how close (despite the previous disclaimer) is the voice of the narrator to that of Cozzens the author? Henry Dodd Worthington is no apologist for James Gould Cozzens. To say that the attributes and concerns of the professional writer are those that are found in Cozzens's own fiction is merely to say that throughout his career Cozzens—who as a professional has more in common with Knox Frothingham than Henry Worthington— eschewed popularity, literary movements, social causes, and political issues in favor of working toward an accurate presentation of human nature operating in a wide variety of conditions and circumstances. Quite aside from his early ambition to be a writer, and the fact that his academic training is in the field of literature, Henry Worthington's concern with writers and writing is understandable from the point of view of a man who is trying to write his own memoirs honestly and truthfully. In telling us the problems he encounters in rendering his life, Worthington tells us about himself, just as he reveals himself when talking about others—Elaine, Judith, Charlotte, and Eunice Van den Arend. By placing his first-person narrator in the role of autobiographer, Cozzens achieves a complex artistic balance; for we are allowed to observe Worthington through the media of two different, but related processes. On the one hand we see him dealing with the events of his life as a character in a novel, and trying to arrive at an understanding of them; on the other hand we see him as the writer of a book in which he is himself the central character, and who is trying to find the most appropriate form for delineating the personality, life, and times of Henry Dodd Worthington.

This is the sort of complexity that is missed by critics who argue that "Worthington's world is a dry one in which protagonists behave a bit like robots: unexpected turns are explained in terms of what went awry, not in terms of emotional behavior or of the darkness of human nature."[6] Such a judgment is surely not in accord even with the relatively small portion of the novel that has been discussed in this essay; and the apparent lack of emotion or deep feeling is deceptive. In his concluding remarks, Worthington states that he "can hope to work no catharsis of pity and terror. I will try to excuse and console myself with the so-evident common truth that bowels unbound by such catharsis seem very apt to be those that reason and good sense were binding, and a diarrhea of factitious feeling . . . can all too regularly result."[7] There is no lack of emotion in *Morning*

Noon and Night. That such a condition might appear to exist is because Henry Worthington goes to great pains to create some order out of an amazing and potentially chaotic welter of feelings and memories. By the time the novel reaches its conclusion, Worthington has performed a highly creative act by presenting us with a gradually unfolding and articulately contemplative version of himself which we then must be able to interpret.

Rather than shunning human nature, Henry Worthington is obsessed with it, especially his own. An unfeeling human nature would have no problem—as Worthington most emphatically does—in dealing with a memory that, unbidden, dredges up unpleasant recollections. "What comes back sharp and clear," Worthington tells us, "is recollection of disagreeable things: mean actions of mine; uglinesses of greed or lust; shameful exhibitions of ignorance; deserved humiliations; mortifying follies and defeats" (pp. 12–13). At times humorously self-deprecating, Worthington has cause to be amazed at how he has ended up:

> Why, who is this 'I' but the pretentious adolescent Hank showing his meager culture off on the beach below the Van den Arend house; who but the literary young collegian pretending to intellectualism . . . but soon proved writer *manqué?* Who but the M.A.-earning prepared instructor in college English so easily put off plans to teach by his evinced alter ego, Judith Conway's pristine marriage bed's libidinous athlete whose life's aim and end seem to be pieces of tail? Who but the highfalutin, hoity-toity assistant to Mr. Garesche in the Boylston Street rathole of an office? Can you imagine such a fellow, all foolishness, frivolity, self-indulgence, and infirmity of purpose ending up great and powerful? [p. 353].

In a world of uncertainty, whose day-to-day events are for the most part unpredictable, it is best to strive for some understanding of the basic principles of human existence, not the ability to predict what individual humans might do in a given situation. By the conclusion of *Morning Noon and Night,* it is clear that Henry Worthington has come to terms with a significant number of these principles. He understands that the man who does the best he can with things as they are is often going to find out that "things" are not what they appear to be. He notes without becoming cynical that people (including himself) are self-serving. He knows the potential treachery in positing cause-and-effect relationships: "Difficulties are added to the work of constructing an account of how things were when what was tremendous can very well, in effect on your life, have been causally immaterial, while what was trivial wasn't immaterial" (p. 399). Success is often a matter of blind luck, or chance—the fortuitous working out of things "that provides that nothing if not good about me shall come out, that no truth to my, or my work's, discredit will ever be brought to light" (p. 66). And finally, in his various comments on writing and on life, Worthington shows a realization that "issues" have little to do with living, and that no amount of sheer fact will ever reveal a necessary truth about the human condition. Henry Worthington's emotional control allows the ironies of his life to be understated, and they are therefore invested with a subtle impact that gathers strength throughout the novel. Rather than being "a hollow papier-maché figure containing the author,"[8] Henry Worthington is for the most part an admirable man who perceives many of the weaknesses that qualify his virtues, and is capable still of functioning positively within his world and of maintaining a solid sense of self-respect.

11

Statements on
James Gould Cozzens

By Malcolm Cowley[1]

The Howells Medal of the Academy is awarded once every five years to a distinguished work of American fiction. This year the lustral honor is being paid to a very distinguished work that has been more disputed over and dissected than any other novel of the period beginning with 1955.

By Love Possessed, published in August 1957, had the early misfortune to be greeted with almost unanimous praise. The physical laws that govern literary opinion are such that anyone might have predicted the sequel: six months later the praise was answered with an equally vehement chorus of abuse. Except when this second chorus, or antistrophe, happened to deal with the debatable question of Mr. Cozzens's style, it was hardly at all concerned with standards. Chiefly the novel was attacked for what it seemed to suggest in terms of political doctrines, group loyalties, ethical imperatives, and the struggle between new and old tendencies in American society.

On all these public or personal questions, the Academy as a body has never taken a stand. Its award of the Howells Medal to James Gould Cozzens does not, I am sure, imply its approval or disapproval of his voting record, which he tells us is Republican, or his choice of characters, which seems to reveal a sympathy with the prosperous Anglo-Saxon segment of the population, or the religious faith of his hero, which is a rather detached Episcopalianism, or even his personal scale of values, with its eighteenth-century distrust of unbridled emotions and its emphasis on understanding and enduring the world that exists. The Academy is honoring a literary work, not a body of opinion.

In the field of literature proper, the award does not imply that the Academy would recommend as a universal practice Mr. Cozzens's method of constructing a novel, which consists in telling an essentially simple fable that observes the classical unities of time, place, and action, while extending the scope of the book by introducing scores of characters and projecting their lives far into the past. The award might imply, however, that nobody has practiced that particular method with more painstaking craftsmanship or a broader understanding of human relations in all their blundering complexity. Reread after three years, *By Love Possessed* appears to be a solid and lasting and, to his fellow novelists, an enviably difficult achievement, that is, a very long novel presenting the events of exactly forty-nine hours as seen through the eyes of a single character, with a whole community involved in a diversity of incidents, and yet with every incident maintaining a single tone and contributing to a single theme, so that the end of the book is foreshadowed in its beginning. The Howells Medal is being awarded to a man who, quite simply and apart from controversy, is the greatest architect in contemporary American fiction.

Outside of his other distinctions, Mr. Cozzens is known for his custom of never answering his critics and never appearing on public occasions. In a letter of acceptance he says: "I am moved by the Academy's vote to honor me. As a token of the consensus of many distinguished members, I accept the Howells Medal with gratitude."

By James Dickey

It has been said that the most difficult of all the prose fictionist's tasks is to create a character who is morally good and interesting as well. There are a few of these, scattered through literature in several languages, but by far the preponderance of haunting characters are men of evil, connivance, weakness, and self-ruin, many through the sin of *hubris*. Somerset Maugham, a more canny judge of fictional characters than is usually supposed, has remarked, for example, on the symbol projected by "the sinister and gigantic figure of Captain Ahab" in *Moby Dick*. Maugham says, "I can think of no creature of fiction that approaches his stature. You must go to the Greek dramatists for anything like that sense of doom with which everything that you are told about him fills you, and to Shakespeare to find beings of such terrible power."

In James Gould Cozzens there are none of these mighty figures of doom. His world is permeated by the efforts of the decent, limited man of good will to make some kind of moral sense, in a social situation, of what other less steadfast and more devious people have let or made happen to it. For example, Colonel Ross in *Guard of Honor* is one such man. Arthur Winner in *By Love Possessed* is another. God knows, these Cozzens characters are not perfect, but they are cast in roles where they must act for the common good, within the Air Force, the law firm, the family: in short, within the social structure where they happen to find themselves, or into which fate has cast them. Human concern, plus a certain know-how—often haphazardly acquired—are presumed to operate in favor of a larger group of men than is comprised by the central character himself. Cozzens is the novelist of a complex decency, and the best one of these that we have. The Colonel Rosses and the Arthur Winners, as limited as they seem, are the human beings who are going to save us, and not the Shakespearean Captain Ahabs who end up by being merely interesting. A difficult decorum, plus a steadfast good will in a limited—sometimes a desperately restricted—and middle-aged human being: *that* is a good man.

And so is Cozzens.

By Orville Prescott

One of the more striking truths about the major American novelists of this century is that they were more notable for their natural talent, their technical innovations in writing, and their emotional force than for their intelligence. Hemingway, Faulkner and Fitzgerald are the most distinguished of these. But one novelist stands alone as the most intelligent American novelist of his time, James Gould Cozzens.

Cozzens began as a clever, ironic, and showy writer. He developed into a coldly objective, awesomely astute, and intellectually illuminating writer. His technique was always fascinating. He looked at the world with a certain disenchantment combined with a sort of Olympian compassion. The result of such unusual attitudes was an array of distinguished novels, of which three rank among the finest ever written in America. These are *The Just and The Unjust, Guard Of Honor* and *By Love Possessed*.

Each of these (and several of his others also) explores a dramatic situation where individual characters are revealed as they are shaped by particular social circumstances: the practice of law, the problems of a great military organization, or the mysteries of love and sex. Readers follow the course of these narratives with absorbed interest, but without emotional involvement, which is why Cozzens has never been very popular with women readers. Readers are almost as interested in the mind of the writer as in the story he is telling. An anthology of Cozzens's comments on life and people would make a stimulating and diverting work. It would contain such remarks as these:

"Doubtless luck is the chief factor, but, dispassionately considered, almost every financially unlucky person is a plain fool to start with" (*The Last Adam*).

"Yes, there'll be more wars; and soon, I don't doubt. There always have been. There'll be deaths, and disappointments and failures. When they come, you meet them. Nobody promises you a good time or an easy time. I don't know who it was who said when we think of the past we regret and when we think of the future we fear. And with reason. But no bets are off. There is a present to think of, and as long as you live there always will be. In the present, every day is a miracle" (*The Just and the Unjust*).

By Joseph Slater

What ought to be in the first volume of the Collected Edition of James Gould Cozzens which some press will some day publish? Not *S.S. San Pedro,* I hope; not even that disinherited little masterpiece, *The Son of Perdition;* but rather the novel Cozzens wrote when he was nineteen—not just because it was his first but because it is surprisingly good and because it reveals less guardedly than his later fiction the intensity of his artistic commitment.

I do not mean to argue—or rather, to assert, since I have too few words for argument—that *Confusion* is a masterpiece of any sort, big or little. Its faults are obvious and even predictable: it is overgrown and gangling; it sometimes freezes, sometimes gushes; its young men are Brooks Brothers mannequins; its young heroine's accidental death, "when death casually wiped a finger across the slate," is thematically irrelevant. But these are youthful faults, minor, endearing, evanescent. What remains in the ear is a prose of often astounding elegance, in the eye a Pissarro Europe and a Childe Hassam New

York, and in the mind the growth and breaking of a girl's spirit. What holds the book's vivid but seemingly incoherent parts together is its concern with education, for *Confusion* is consciously and consistently a *Bildungsroman.* The girl Cerise moves from the certainties of a sailboat and a horse, fencing and a yacht on the Danube, through tutoring in history and languages to a girls' school in Connecticut and the confusions of religion, sex, love, duty, art, and calling. At the end, everything is empty and `confounded, and the marriage to which she is fleeing would have been another confusion. To extricate her by two casual movements of death's finger was an artistic mistake, no doubt. But the final scenes of the novel have been so painful, so clearly a nightmare of the youthful author himself, that he could hardly have let his heroine survive into a lifetime of triviality and failure. Not at nineteen.

Cerise is a credible and touching portrait of a young lady. She is also, I suspect, a kind of self-portrait. As literary as Stephen Dedalus, she is even more bookish. At Brentano's she buys, greedily, sensuously, "Shelton in lovely green leather, Adlington and Malory . . . and *Purchas Pilgrimes* with their fat bindings and generous type." The built-in bookcases of her study overflow, glow "with gilt lettered content," and she takes down an Elizabethan volume to taste again "the remembered lusciousness of phrase." She sees beauty as redemptive; she wants to create it, like the jeweler she visits on Christmas Eve. In her passion for "the swift sinuous grace of wording" and her "fierce desire to write," she tells us more about the boy Cozzens once was than that very private man is ever likely to do.

By C. P. Snow

James Gould Cozzens is one of the best realistic novelists ever produced by America. By "realistic" here I mean something different from naturalistic. American opinion has tended to be more sympathetic to naturalistic or symbolic novels than to realistic one. When realistic novelists have emerged, as with Cozzens, they haven't been understood or cherished as they deserve.

It would be good if all Professors of English read James R. Kincaid's leading article ("Bring Back *The Trollopian*," [June 1967]) in *Nineteenth-Century Fiction.* In this he says that it is easy for academic criticism to come to terms with Henry James and nowadays fairly easy with Dickens. But we need a completely new kind of academic criticism to help us read Tolstoy as he should be read. In precisely the same sense there is no existing academic criticism which helps us to read Cozzens. It would be good to think that one was now in the process of emerging.

By Edward Weeks

I am happy to learn that you are editing a volume of essays in appreciation of James Gould Cozzens. As you may know, the *Atlantic* published his first article, "A Democratic School," in 1920, written while Cozzens was a student at Kent School.

I read all of his early novels and reviewed some of them. He was a fastidious craftsman, rewriting and polishing, and as I suspect, never quite satisfied with the final result. Through my friendship with his wife, Bernice Baumgarten, one of the most trustworthy of literary agents, I learned of the unsparing dedication that consumed the long intervals between his major novels.

The two that most appealed to me are *Guard of Honor,* which is surely one of the finest novels of World War II, a large-scale, very busy, very masculine story, confined to three tense days at a big air base in Florida in 1943. The four men, "Bus" Beal, the youngest Major General in the Air Force; Colonel Ross, the judge; Captain Nathaniel Hicks, and the convalescent fighter pilot, Carricker, are the bright strong strands who hold the diffuse story together.

Seven years' work went into Cozzens' finest novel, *By Love Possessed,* and again it is a spacious story, shuttling back and forth through exactly forty-nine hours in the life of Arthur Winner, the leading lawyer in a small town in Pennsylvania, the current of whose personality sweeps the reader forward. Love in its many different aspects is the theme of this fine book, and in our present period when sex has been so continually distorted in fiction, it is refreshing to remember the loyalty, the compassion, and the passion which Arthur Winner feels for those who come close to him.

By Jerome Weidman

James Gould Cozzens's first novel, *Confusion,* was published by the B. J. Brimmer Company, Boston, in 1924. I read the book in 1926. The delay was due to circumstances beyond my control.

In 1926 I had not yet learned that books can be purchased in shops like shoes and Indian nuts. This was just as well. In 1926 I had no money with which to pay for anything, not even my own Indian nuts.

In 1926 I obtained all my reading matter for free from the Hamilton Fish Park Branch of the New York Public Library. It was a very good library. However, depending as it did on a central bureaucracy somewhere uptown for what it was able to place on its shelves, the Hamilton Fish Park or My Branch did not have the opportunity to offer *Confusion* to its card holders until 1926. As a result of the gap between the 1924 publication of *Confusion* and my 1926 encounter with the book, I suffered no discomfort.

For one thing, I was unaware of the gap. I had not yet learned how to find the publication date of a book by examining the back of the title page. For another, I had never before read anything by James Gould Cozzens. Not many people had. It was, as I have indicated, his first book. I had not yet, therefore, suffered an impatience with which I have now lived for half a century: waiting for Cozzens's next book.

There is a third reason why I was cushioned from the small trauma that might have been caused by my delay in putting my hands on a copy of *Confusion*. In 1926 I had other things on my mind. It was my bar mitzvah year. Once I got over that I was free to get on with other things. These included the work of James Gould Cozzens.

I am not a professional literary critic. By which I mean I have never been paid to deliver, in print or from a platform, an opinion about the work of any writer, living or dead. I do not mean to imply that in this area I am mute. On a clear day, if you keep your window open, you can probably hear me. I do not say you should. I mean only that, like most human beings, I have opinions. If not like most, then certainly like many, I am not bashful about expressing them. I am, however, cautious about doing so to strangers. Many of them, I have found over the years, are bigger than I am. So are many of my friends, but all of these have been chosen with care, so I feel reasonably certain that none of those I have left will respond to one of my literary opinions with violence. Even when I repeat them. Over the years the American novelist about whom I have repeated my opinion with the greatest frequency is James Gould Cozzens. The reason is simple.

Since 1926, when I read the first of the fourteen Cozzens books I now have on my shelf, he has never let me down. He is one of only two writers now working in English who, in my private record book, have chalked up this enviable score.

I could explain here, because I have done it many times elsewhere, what it is about these two writers that I find as satisfying on the second or twenty-second reading as I found on the first. The explanation is not very satisfactory. Not even to me. So I am not going to repeat it here. I will instead lean on a few words by a man who has written his share of good ones.

"I wanted," Hemingway once stated in a fragment of autobiography, "to put words down in such a way that they would not go bad in the end."

An admirable mark to shoot at. In my time as a reader, from the Hamilton Fish Park Branch of the New York Public Library until today, no American novelist has for me hit this mark so consistently as James Gould Cozzens.

Notes

The Publications of
James Gould Cozzens

Notes

1. The Complex World of James Gould Cozzens

1. *American Literature,* 27 (May 1955), 157–71.

2. James Gould Cozzens: The Condition of Modern Man

1. *American Scholar,* 27 (Winter 1957–58), 92–99.

3. Cozzens and the Conservative Spirit

1. "James Gould Cozzens: The Condition of Modern Man," *American Scholar,* 27 (Winter 1957–58), 92–99. Reprinted in this volume.
2. "Controversy," *American Scholar,* 27 (Winter 1957–58), 229.
3. No mention shall be made here of *Castaway* (1934), a remarkable novel, at once a modern Robinson Crusoe tale and a Kafkaesque fantasy; of *Ask Me Tomorrow* (1940), a rather unsuccessful book because of the fuzziness of its themes and the uncertain handling of the setting; and of *Morning Noon and Night,* Cozzens's latest novel (1968), which, though in a different setting, tackles many of the themes already developed in earlier works.
4. London: Cambridge University Press, 1965.
5. Ibid, p. 336.
6. Ibid, p. 361.
7. Richard M. Ludwig, "A Reading of the James Gould Cozzens Manuscripts," *The Princeton University Library Chronicle,* 19 (Autumn 1957), 7.
8. New York: Harcourt, Brace, 1957, p. 118.
9. "Notes on a Difficulty of Law by One Unlearned in It," *Bucks County Law Reporter,* 1 (1951), 302.
10. D. E. S. Maxwell, *Cozzens* (Edinburgh & London: Oliver & Boyd, 1964), p. 1.
11. See Pierre Michel, *James Gould Cozzens* (New York: Twayne, 1974), pp. 137–49.
12. The later style enhances the quality of *Guard of Honor* because Cozzens remains precise and to the point; in *By Love Possessed* and *Morning Noon and Night,* however, those mannerisms, sometimes, tend to be used for their own sake (compare, for instance, p. 527 in *Guard of Honor* and p. 519 in *By Love Possessed*).

4. Moral Realism: The Development of an Attitude

1. Some of the material in this essay appeared in a different form in "The Commitment of James Gould Cozzens," *Arizona Quarterly,* 16 (Summer 1960), 129–43.

2. Ernest Hemingway, *A Farewell to Arms* (New York: Scribners, 1929), p. 350. *The Just and the Unjust* (New York: Harcourt, Brace, 1942), p. 434.

3. James Gould Cozzens as interviewed by Robert Van Gelder, "James Gould Cozzens at Work," *New York Times Book Review* (23 June 1940), p. 14. Mr. Cozzens has stated in a letter to me, 14 March 1956, "I made the mistake of letting myself be talked into an interview (my last) and nothing I was reported to have said had any significance of any kind." This would seem to undercut to a great extent my speculations based on this interview, but I have allowed them to stand for two reasons: first, they are supported by the evidence of the books themselves; and second, it is possible that Mr. Cozzens's denial is excessively sweeping.

4. Ibid., p. 14.

5. *Confusion* (Boston: Brimmer, 1924), p. 211. Shortly before the end of the story Pelton, the other godfather, feels this, too. He remembers "a December noon when Tischoifsky had talked to him. He had laughed then, and now for the first time he began to wonder if Leon had been right. Over-educated sensibilities. . . . ," p. 344.

6. *Michael Scarlett* (New York: Boni, 1925), pp. 158–59.

7. *Cock Pit* (New York: Morrow, 1928), pp. 168–70.

8. *The Son of Perdition* (New York: Morrow, 1929), pp. 132–33.

9. "The Master of the Vestris," *Nation* 127 (28 November 1928), 570.

10. Letter to Scholes, 14 March 1956. Cozzens added that he "went once and looked at Vestris's sister ship in Hoboken."

11. *S.S. San Pedro* (New York: Harcourt, Brace, 1931), p. 24.

12. *Castaway* (New York: Random House, 1934), pp. 180–81.

13. Stanley Edgar Hyman, "James Gould Cozzens and the Art of the Possible," *New Mexico Quarterly Review,* 19 (Winter 1949), 479.

14. Henry James, "The Limitations of Dickens," *Views and Reviews* (Boston: Ball, 1908) p. 160.

15. This is admitted by Cozzens, who would perhaps dismiss all his short stories too readily. In his 14 March 1956 letter to me he said of his short stories, "The form never interested me and I quit it as soon as I stopped needing a fast few hundred dollars." The twenty-one stories are: "Lions are Lower Today" (1930), "Some Day You'll Be Sorry" (1930), "October Occupancy" (1930), "We'll Recall it with Affection" (1930), "The Guns of the Enemy" (1930), "Fortune and Men's Eyes" (1931), "Farewell to Cuba" (1931), "The Way to Go Home" (1931), "Every Day's a Holiday" (1933), "My Love to Marcia" (1934), "Love Leaves Town" (1934), "Straight Story" (1934), "Success Story" (1935), "Foot in It" (1935), "Total Stranger" (1936), "Whose Broad Stripes and Bright Stars" (1936), "Something About a Dollar" (1936), "The Animals' Fair" (1937), "Child's Play" (1937), "Men Running" (1937), "Son and Heir" (1938).

16. Edward Wilson Parmelee, "A Boarding School Inquiry," *Atlantic Monthly,* 125 (January 1920), 99.

17. James Gould Cozzens, "A Democratic School," *Atlantic Monthly,* 125 (March 1920), 383–84.

18. "Of Youth and Age: James Gould Cozzens," *Pacific Spectator,* 5 (Winter 1951), 48–62).

19. Van Gelder, "James Gould Cozzens at Work." The "Summer Soldier" was finally published in 1942 as *The Just and the Unjust.*

5. *The Title of* The Last Adam

1. The first edition published by Harcourt, Brace (New York, 1933) is textually superseded by the paperbound Harvest Books (HB–12) edition (New York: Harcourt, Brace & World, 1956) in its later printings, which, beginning with the fifth printing (E.10.60), contain authorial emendations. The Harvest edition is the source for my quotations. All subsequent references to it are provided in parentheses.

2. *James Gould Cozzens: An Annotated Checklist* (Kent, OH: Kent State University Press, 1971).

3. "A Reading of the James Gould Cozzens Manuscripts," *Princeton University Library Chronicle*, 19 (Autumn 1957), 9.

4. Unpublished letter, 9 December 1976.

5. *The Works of Thomas Hood* 6 (London: Moxon, 1871), 415.

6. Letter to Cass, 9 December 1976.

7. For example, Edward Weeks thought it "easy to like," thought it interested him "more by variety and surprise than by steady development" (*Atlantic Monthly*, 151 [February 1933], 14). Herschel Brickell considered it "excellent . . . realistic," but lacking "the overtones, perhaps, that go into still better fiction" (*North American Review*, 235 [March 1933], 282–83). Helen MacAfee wrote, "If narrative energy and a large fund of miscellaneous information could combine to make a great novel, we should have one in *The Last Adam* . . . but unrestrained reporting of minutiae . . . clogs attention" when facts are "without the intimations of perception and feeling that facts in a well-directed novel should impart. . ." (*Yale Review*, 22 [Spring 1933], 6). T. S. Matthews, calling Cozzens "a non-serious novelist," found the book entertaining "as gossip—which is what it is" (*New Republic*, 73 [25 January 1933], 301–02). William B. Ober admired its "Honest craftsmanship," but found that "its scope is small"; he sought "additional qualities before bestowing accolades" (*Carleton Miscellany*, 4 [Fall 1963], 105). Alvah C. Bessie, discouraged by "slick, polished, well-written, interesting but invariably empty novels," categorized *The Last Adam* as "just such a novel," implying that "ill-digested details were introduced with the implicit intention of camouflaging an absence of substance" ("Connecticut Town," *Saturday Review of Literature*, 9 [21 January 1933], 389).

8. *The Novels of James Gould Cozzens* (New York: Harcourt, Brace, 1959), pp. 111–12.

9. "The Conflicts of Reality: Cozzens' *The Last Adam*," in *Seven Contemporary Authors: Essays on Cozzens, Miller, West, Golding, Heller, Albee, and Powers*, ed. Thomas B. Whitbread (Austin: University of Texas Press, 1966).

10. Ibid., p. 19.

11. *The Novels of James Gould Cozzens*, p. 37.

12. "The Conflicts of Reality," p. 14.

13. *James Gould Cozzens* (New York: Twayne, 1974), p. 40.

14. G. Clifton Bingham, "Love's Old Sweet Song," *Vocal Blossoms*, 1st ser., No. 67 (New York: Century Music Publishing Co., n.d.).

15. *James Gould Cozzens* (Minneapolis: University of Minnesota Press, 1966), p. 14.

16. *James Gould Cozzens: Novelist of Intellect* (Pittsburgh: University of Pittsburgh Press, 1963), p. 29.

17. *The Novels of James Gould Cozzens*, p. 37.

18. "The Conflicts of Reality," p. 14.
19. "James Gould Cozzens: A Cultural Dilemma," in *Essays in Modern American Literature,* ed. Richard E. Langford, Stetson Studies in Humanities, No. 1 (Deland, FL: Stetson University Press, 1963), p. 105.
20. 28 July 1976.
21. Robert Van Felder, "James Gould Cozzens at Work," *New York Times Book Review* (23 June 1940), p. 14; William Du Bois, "Recluse," *New York Times Book Review* (25 August 1957), p. 8.
22. Unpublished letter, 7 August 1976.
23. "The Conflicts of Reality," p. 21.
24. J. Murray, "Adam," *The New Bible Dictionary,* ed. J. D. Douglas, et al. (Grand Rapids, MI: Eerdmans, 1962).
25. W. H. Monk, "Victory," *The Hymnal of the Protestant Episcopal Church in the United States of America* (Greenwich, CT: Seabury Press, 1940), Hymn no. 91, vss. 1, 5.
26. G. J. Elvey, "Diademata," *The Hymnal of the Protestant Episcopal Church in the United States of America* (Greenwich, CT: Seabury Press, 1940), Hymn no. 352, vss. 1, 3.
27. *James Gould Cozzens,* p. 40.
28. *The Novels of James Gould Cozzens,* p. 134.

6. *Providental Luck in a Hard-Luck World*

1. Richard M. Ludwig, "A Reading of the James Gould Cozzens Manuscripts," *Princeton University Library Chronicle,* 19 (Autumn 1957), 1–12.
2. *Guard of Honor* (New York: Harcourt, Brace, 1948), p. 534.
3. Ludwig, p. 6.
4. *Essays Second Series,* Centenary Edition (Boston & New York: Houghton, Mifflin, 1876), pp. 69–70.
5. Pragmatism (Cambridge, MA: Harvard University Press, 1975), p. 138.
6. *Book-of-the-Month Club News* (September 1948), p. 9.

8. *The Novelist as Professional*

1. *Harper's Magazine,* 198 (February 1949), 70–73. Copyright © 1949 by *Harper's Magazine.* Copyright renewed 1977. By permission of Mr. Bernard DeVoto.

9. *Nomination for a Nobel Prize*

1. *Harper's Magazine,* 215 (September 1957), 14–15, 18, 20.

10. *Henry Dodd Worthington*

1. *Morning Noon and Night* (New York: Harcourt, Brace & World, 1968), p. 3. Subsequent references to this novel appear in the text.
2. The kind of contemplative and philosophical discourse sustained by Worthington in *Morning Noon and Night* is prefigured in the monologues of Julius

Penrose in *By Love Possessed* (New York: Harcourt, Brace, 1957). See, e.g., pp. 214–42 and pp. 543–65.

3. "The Complex World of James Gould Cozzens," *American Literature,* 27 (1955), 157.

4. See, e.g., the following reviews: Howard Junker, *Newsweek,* 72 (26 August 1968), 86, 86D; Stanley Kauffman, *Atlantic Monthly,* 222 (September 1968), 119–21; Edwin J. Kenney, *Nation,* 207 (9 September 1968), 218–20; and John Updike, *New Yorker,* 44 (2 November 1968), 197–201.

5. What Johnson actually wrote was, "Nothing can please many, and please long, but just representations of general nature." See "Preface to Shakespeare, 1765," in Arthur Sherbo, ed., *The Yale Edition of the Works of Samuel Johnson: Johnson on Shakespeare,* 7 (New Haven: Yale University Press), 61.

6. Pierre Michel, *James Gould Cozzens* (New York: Twayne, 1974), p. 130.

7. *Morning Noon and Night,* p. 404. Cf. *Ask Me Tomorrow* (New York: Harcourt, Brace, 1940), p. 68, where Francis Ellery, a young novelist, finds himself in a position where he feels he must exercise strict discipline over his emotions: "The mingling of pity . . . of the sense of things gone, of the unfairness of fate, of disappointment, of disillusion; perhaps, of the hour of death and the day of judgment, all thrust toward the bowels of his compassion. They were bowels not particularly easy to get at; but, on close inspection, were they any different or any decenter than the man of sensibility's bellyful? Eviscerated, gushing freely out, all bowels looked alike. . . ."

8. Kaufmann, p. 120.

11. Statements

1. Reprinted from the *Proceedings* of the American Academy of Arts and Letters and the National Institute of Arts and Letters, Number 11, 1961.

The Publications of James Gould Cozzens

Books

Confusion. Boston: Brimmer, 1924. Novel.

Michael Scarlett. New York: Boni, 1925; London: Holden, 1927. Novel.

Cock Pit. New York: Morrow, 1928. Novel.

The Son of Perdition. New York: Morrow, 1929. London: Longmans, Green, 1929. Novel.

S.S. San Pedro. New York: Harcourt, Brace, 1931. London: Longmans, Green, 1931. Novel.

The Last Adam. New York: Harcourt, Brace, 1933. Republished as *A Cure of Flesh.* London: Longmans, Green, 1933. Novel.

Castaway. London: Longmans, Green, 1934. New York: Random House, 1934. Novel.

Men and Brethren. New York: Harcourt, Brace, 1936; London: Longmans, Green, 1936. Novel.

Ask Me Tomorrow. New York: Harcourt, Brace, 1940; London: Longmans, Green, 1940. Novel.

The Just and the Unjust. New York: Harcourt, Brace, 1942; London: Cape, 1943. Novel.

Guard of Honor. New York: Harcourt, Brace, 1948; London: Longmans, Green, 1949. Novel.

By Love Possessed. New York: Harcourt, Brace, 1957; London: Longmans, Green, 1958. Novel.

Children and Others. New York: Harcourt, Brace & World, 1964; London: Longmans, Green, 1965. Short stories.

Morning Noon and Night. New York: Harcourt, Brace & World, 1968; London: Longmans, Green, 1968. Novel.

A Flower in Her Hair. Bloomfield Hills, MI & Columbia, SC: Bruccoli Clark, 1974. Short story.

A Rope for Dr. Webster. Bloomfield Hills, MI & Columbia, SC: Bruccoli Clark, 1976. Essay.

Just Representations A James Gould Cozzens Reader, ed. Matthew J. Bruccoli. Carbondale & Edwardsville: Southern Illinois University Press; New York & London: Harcourt Brace Jovanovich, 1978.

Some Putative Facts of Hard Record. New York & London: Harcourt Brace Jovanovich; Carbondale & Edwardsville: Southern Illinois University Press, 1978.

Contributions to Periodicals

This list omits published letters and interviews

"The Andes," *The Quill* [Staten Island Academy] 30 (January 1915), 5. Poem.

"A Democratic School" *Atlantic,* 125 (March 1920), 383–84. Article.

"The Trail of the Lakes," *Kent Quarterly,* 12 (May 1920), 86–91. Essay.

"A Friendly Thinker," *Kent Quarterly,* 13 (December 1920), 13–14. Essay.

"Good Old Main Street," *Kent Quarterly,* 13 (March 1921), 40–42. Essay.

"Religion for Beginners: A Nova Scotian Sketch," *Kent Quarterly,* 14 (December 1921), 25–28. Short story.

"A Study in the Art of the Novel," *Kent Quarterly,* 14 (July 1922), 77–79. Essay.

"The Trust in Princes," *Harvard Advocate* 109 (November 1, 1922), 44. Poem.

Review of *The Bright Shawl,* by Joseph Hergesheimer, *Harvard Advocate,* 109 (December 1, 1922), 85–86.

"Where Angels Fear to Tread," *Harvard Advocate,* 109 (December 1, 1922), 86. Poem.

"The Passing," *Harvard Advocate,* 109 (January 1, 1923), 121. Poem.

Review of *Don Rodriguez: Chronicles of Shadow Valley,* by Lord Dunsany, *Harvard Advocate,* 109 (January 1, 1923), 120–21.

"Condolence," *Harvard Advocate,* 109 (February 1, 1923), 151. Poem.

Review of *Love and Freindship,* by Jane Austen, *Harvard Advocate,* 109 (April 7, 1923), 291.

"The Virginia Rose: A Ballad for Eunice," *Harvard Advocate,* 109 (May 1, 1923), 338–39. Poem.

"Two Arts," *Harvard Advocate,* 109 (May 1, 1923), 347. Poem.

"For a Motet by Josquin de Pres," *Harvard Advocate,* 109 (June 1, 1923), 404. Poem.

"Remember the Rose," *Harvard Advocate,* 109 (June 1, 1923), 395–97. Short story.

"The Long Elusion," *Casements* [Brown University], July 1923 (unpaged). Poem.

"Romanesque," Kent Quarterly, 15 (July 1923), 85. Poem.

"ΑΦΡΟΛΙΤΗΚΥΠΡΙΑ," *Kent Quarterly,* 15 (July 1923), 91. Poem.

"Hail and Farewell," *Harvard Advocate,* 110 (October 1, 1923), 13. Poem.

"Blue Seas," *Palms,* 1 (Autumn 1923), 110. Poem.

Review of *The Shepherd's Pipe,* by Arthur Schnitzler, *Dial,* 75 (December 1923), 608–10. Signed Cuthbert Wright, but written by Cozzens at Wright's request.

"Abishag," *Linonia,* 1 (June 1925), 45–53. Short story.

"The Point of View," *Kent Quarterly,* 17 (June 1925), 55–59. Essay.

"Harvard Author Reviews New Work 'The History of Michael Scarlett,'" *Daily Princetonian,* 46 (June 12, 1925), 1, 4.

"A Letter to a Friend," *Pictorial Review,* 27 (May 1926), 16, 116, 117. Short story.

"Notes from the Club Library," *Winged Foot* [New York Athletic Club], 38 (September 1927), 29–30. Review.

"Notes from the Club Library," *Winged Foot,* 38 (October 1927), 17. Review.

"The Library Talk for the Month," *Winged Foot,* 38 (November 1927), 28–29. Review.

"Notes from the Club Library," *Winged Foot,* 38 (December 1927), 42. Review.

"Notes from the Club Library," *Winged Foot,* 39 (January 1928), 20–21. Review.

"Future Assured," *Saturday Evening Post,* 202 (November 2, 1929), 22–23, 116, 120, 121, 124. Short story.

"The Defender of Liberties," *Alhambra,* 1 (January 1930), 14–17, 54, 55, 56. Short story.

"Lions are Lower Today," *Saturday Evening Post,* 202 (February 15, 1930), 36, 38, 40, 154, 158. Short story.

"Some Day You'll Be Sorry," *Saturday Evening Post,* 202 (June 21, 1930), 44, 47, 60, 63, 64, 66. Short story.

"October Occupancy," *American Magazine,* 110 (October 1930), 56–59, 153, 154, 155, 156, 157, 158. Short story.

"We'll Recall It with Affection," *Saturday Evening Post,* 203 (October 4, 1930), 12–13, 149, 150, 152, 153, 154. Short story.

"The Guns of the Enemy," *Saturday Evening Post,* 203 (November 1, 1930), 12–13, 74–77, 78, 80, 82. Short story.

"Fortune and Men's Eyes," *Woman's Home Companion,* 58 (February 1931), 29–30, 134, 138, 140. Short story.

"Thoughts Brought on by 633 Manuscripts," *Bookman,* 73 (June 1931), 381–84. Essay.

"Farewell to Cuba," *Scribner's,* 90 (November 1931), 533–44. Short story.

"The Way to Go Home," *Saturday Evening Post,* 204 (December 26, 1931), 12–13, 59, 60. Short story.

"Kent, a New School," *Town & Country,* 88 (August 1, 1933), 38–41, 57. Article.

"Every Day's a Holiday," *Scribner's,* 94 (December 1933), 339–44. Short story.

"My Love to Marcia," *Collier's,* 93 (March 3, 1934), 16–17, 46, 47. Short story.

"Love Leaves Town," *American Magazine,* 118 (September 1934), 24–27, 119, 120, 121. Short story.

"Straight Story," *Collier's,* 94 (November 17, 1934), 22. Short story.

"Success Story," *Collier's,* 95 (April 20, 1935), 26. Short story.

"Foot in It," *Redbook,* 65 (August 1935), 28–29. Reprinted as "Clerical Error." Short story.

"Total Stranger," *Saturday Evening Post,* 208 (February 15, 1936), 8–9, 96, 98, 100. Short story.

"Whose Broad Stripes and Bright Stars," *Saturday Evening Post,* 208 (May 23, 1936), 16–17, 69, 71. Short story.

"Something about a Dollar," *Saturday Evening Post,* 209 (August 15, 1936), 27–28, 62, 64. Short story.

Foreword to *Kent Quarterly,* 1 (November 26, 1936), 3–4.

"The Animals' Fair," *Saturday Evening Post,* 209 (January 16, 1937), 18–19, 47, 50, 53, 54. Short story.

"Child's Play," *Saturday Evening Post,* 209 (February 13, 1937), 16–17, 61, 63, 65. Short story.

"Men Running," *Atlantic,* 160 (July 1937), 81–91. Short story.

"Son and Heir," *Saturday Evening Post,* 210 (April 2, 1938), 10–11, 86, 88, 89, 91. Short story.

"The Fuller Brush Co.," *Fortune,* 18 (October 1938), 69–72, 100, 102, 104. (Although this piece was unsigned, it appeared very much as Cozzens had written it.) Article.

"What They're Reading," *Air Force,* 26 (June 1943), 28. Article.

"Airways Flying," *Air Transport,* 1 (September 1943), 39–42. By Cozzens and Bert Moore. Article.

"The Air Force Training Program," *Fortune,* 29 (February 1944), 147–52. Article drafted by William Vogel and revised by Cozzens.
Review of *The Eagle in the Egg,* by Oliver La Farge, *New York Times Book Review,* (July 24, 1949), pp. 1, 17.
"Notes on a Difficulty of Law by One Unlearned in It," *Bucks County Law Reporter* [Doylestown, PA], 1 (November 15, 1951), 3–7. Essay.
Review of *Reflections on Hanging,* by Arthur Koestler, *Harvard Law Review,* 71 (May 1958), 1377–81.
"One Hundred Ladies," *Saturday Evening Post,* 237 (July 11, 1964), 40, 42, 43, 45, 46, 47. Short story.
"*Candida* by Bernard Shaw," *Saturday Evening Post,* 237 (July 25, 1964), 50, 52, 54, 57. Short story.

Selected Contributions to Books and Pamphlets

"The Class History," *Kent School Year Book 1922.*
"Breaking the Day in Cuba," *Morrow's Almanack for the Year of Our Lord 1929,* ed. Burton Rascoe (New York: Morrow, 1928).
"Portrait of a Chief Officer on His Birthday," *Morrow's Almanack and Every-Day Book for 1930,* ed. Thayer Hobson (New York: Morrow, 1929).
Introduction to *Balzac's Masterpieces* (Philadelphia: McKay, 1931).
"FHS: A Faith that Did Not Fail," *Father Sill's Birthday, March 10, 1956* . . . (Kent, CT: Committee for Kent School's 50th Anniversary Celebration, 1956).
Foreword to *Roses of Yesterday,* by Dorothy Stemler and Nanae Ito (Kansas City, MO: Hallmark, 1967).
Standards Cadet Handbook of Composition (United States Air Force Academy, 1967?). Excerpt from training bulletin.
Introduction to *James Gould Cozzens: A Checklist,* by James B. Meriwether (Detroit: Gale, 1972).

Books & Pamphlets on James Gould Cozzens

Bracher, Frederick. *The Novels of James Gould Cozzens.* New York: Harcourt, Brace, 1959.
Hicks, Granville. *James Gould Cozzens.* Minneapolis: University of Minnesota Press, 1966.
Maxwell, D. E. S. *Cozzens.* Edinburgh & London: Oliver & Boyd, 1964.
Meriwether, James B. *James Gould Cozzens: A Checklist.* Detroit: Bruccoli Clark/Gale, 1972.
Michel, Pierre. *James Gould Cozzens.* New York: Twayne, 1974.
Michel, Pierre. *James Gould Cozzens: An Annotated Checklist.* Kent, OH: Kent State University Press, 1971.
Mooney, Harry John, Jr. *James Gould Cozzens: Novelist of Intellect.* Pittsburgh: University of Pittsburgh Press, 1963.
See also *Critique,* 1 (Winter 1958). James Gould Cozzens number.